I0465674

THE ABC OF
REAL ESTATE
IN INDIA

BY
SACHIN MITTAL

White Falcon
Publishing

www.whitefalconpublishing.com

The ABC of Real Estate In India
Sachin Mittal

www.whitefalconpublishing.com

ISBN - 978-93-87193-16-1

PREFACE

Real Estate is a sector with vast potential which tremendously contributes to the Indian economy. Surprisingly, every man's common dream of owning a house directly connects to the real estate sector.

The idea for this book culminated from the point that there was a dire need of a written work on real estate knowledge comprehended in layman's language.

There was a need for a book which would provide basic information of the vast realty sector in the simplest form, validated with market reports and quotes from the realty experts.

This book 'ABC of Real Estate in India' in general discusses the foundation, dynamics and marketing aspects of the real estate sector and takes purview of the entire industry.

There is also an equal focus on the customer's point of view and an expert analysis of the customer-industry bond. Perhaps, this and many other aspects are inculcated in the book to clarify the importance of the industry in the by lanes of the Indian economy.

This is a humble effort from my side to analyze and assimilate information on the real estate sector and present it before you. It is also important to bring to your notice that the following series of the book will have subsequent volumes in the coming times.

I am highly indebted to the major IPCs (International Property Consultants), market gurus and experts for assisting me while I was writing this book. I want to extend my warm and heartfelt wishes to the readers and hope that they will enjoy and benefit from this book.

Happy Reading!
Sachin Mittal

CONTENTS

ABOUT THE AUTHOR

Sachin Mittal is the new face of finance in today's fast-paced, competitive business environment. Having studied both engineering and arts, Sachin has established himself and built a formidable reputation as a financial wizard. His early career in the finance sector propelled him to become a well-known financial analyst in a mere 10 years.

His foray into the world of finance brought him in contact with the big-wigs of the business and finance sector and his interactions with them sharpened his financial skills and enhanced his business acumen, especially in financial dealings.

His experiences soon brought the realization that in order to succeed in today's business environment, it was necessary to shift from the old, outdated models of money and finance and adopt new techniques in keeping with the ever-changing, fast-paced, new business age.

Sachin operates globally and his business success is as much an outcome of his business and financial acumen as it is of his ability to adapt to changing circumstances. He is a true representative of today's open economy and with his vision and business perspective has carved an admirable and enviable position for himself in the world of business.

Sachin has authored a book Rewriting Kismet where from his own experience he recounts the obstacles and impediments that crop up in any entrepreneur's passage through the tough world of business and commerce.

PART 1

KEY DRIVERS FOR REAL ESTATE GROWTH IN INDIA

CHAPTER I

"Real estate cannot be lost or stolen, nor can it be carried away. Purchased with common sense, paid for in full and managed with reasonable care, it is one of the safest investments in the world."

This quote from Franklin D. Roosevelt, the 32nd President of the United States, sums up the benefits of investing in real estate in mere two sentences. But coming up with the conclusion that real estate is indeed the best form of investment, requires you to understand the different facets of this industry, how they unify and finally, how they work together to bring benefits to the investor.

The modern financial world is intriguing and equally intimidating. With the different types of investment options such as stocks, bonds, mutual funds, gold, etc. it can be very difficult for an investor to not make a mistake, especially, since each of these options are advertised as the key to instant profits. Over the years, we have heard innumerable success as well as failure stories of people who have invested in the above-mentioned options. But the number of success stories are far too low as compared to the ones that met with undesirable results. And for some, the outcome took on a lot more than they ever imagined.

But with the right amount of knowledge and information, investing can transform into one of the most beneficial endeavours of your life.

Investing in real estate, particularly in India, has proven time and again that it is actually an excellent vehicle for building wealth, only if you are a savvy investor.

And, while it is believed that most of the common investment opportunities are all connected to each other in one way or the other, real estate has proven to be a rewarding asset in any and every market condition.

Take the example of the year 2011, when the Sensex fell to almost 25%, the cost of houses in a large majority of Indian cities still remained firm, even when the clouds of economic uncertainty were looming over domestic as well as global markets. In the same year, the cost of properties in 9 out of 15 cities that were covered in Residex (National Housing Banks Residential Index) rose from 4% to 8%. On the other hand, if you would have invested in real estate company stocks, there was a significant possibility that your investment would have reduced by 50% between the time period of December 2010 and December 2011.

Moreover, as per the Indian Brand Equity Foundation Report,

 the real estate market in India will be touching $180 billion by the year 2020 and the housing sector alone will contribute about 5% to 6% to the GDP of the country.

And, it isn't just the predictions for the future, but the development of this sector in the last 10 years alone, is a clear sign which indicates that the real estate sector is further set to grow and rise in the years to come.

EVERYDAY ON THE WAY TO WORK...

You and I are bombarded with compelling advertisements about upcoming real estate projects. It's out there. The large hoardings call out to you, asking you to choose a better home and in turn a better lifestyle. At its core, real estate is both a driver and signifier of growth in any particular region. A common instance being, a housing project uplifting a previously indisposed land or locality. Inherently, real estate assures a better lifestyle for those who choose to buy or rent as well as to those who live around the development property.

It's easy to come across statements in the news like 'the Indian real estate market is expected to touch USD 180 billion by 2020' and 'The housing sector alone contributes 5-6 per cent to the country's Gross Domestic Product (GDP)'. But, what do these statements mean to an average person like you and me? It means India has evolved into the leading destination for real estate business globally and it has become much better than what it used to be.

No, the real estate sector isn't collapsing due to either increasing costs of financing or even the complicated regulatory mechanism as suggested by skeptics who believe in the 'Indian Property Bubble'.

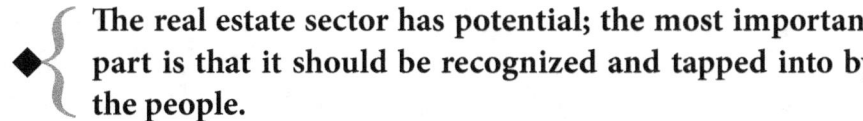

The real estate sector has potential; the most important part is that it should be recognized and tapped into by the people.

A VERY LONG TIME AGO...

In the founding years, 1956 land reforms and a determined emphasis on housing policies led to a steady growth of accommodation in the urban areas as the population grew.

A variety of legislative acts as well as the setting up of the National Housing Policy, the National Building Plan and the Regional Housing Board all contributed positively to the growth of real estate in India.

One major problem was that it lacked the characteristics of an organized sector. It was because of this reason that its growth was stunted since it attracted less organized investment from domestic and external finance institutions. The other problems surrounding it were endless – unorganized dealing, no centralized title registration or guarantee, lack of financing, high transfer taxes, it goes on and on.

The predominant complaint about the real estate sector was *"It is not a transparent industry."* Increasing interest rates were inhibiting buyers and no uniformity among laws in the region added to their inhibitions.

Understanding the need of the hour, several steps were taken for the promotion of transparency and reliability. The first big leap in this aspect was the annulling of the Urban Land (Ceiling and Regulation) Act of 1976 in the year of 1999. Very simply put, this Act barred development on large tracts of land in order to create social equality and prevent hoarding of land available in the market.

 In order to prevent landlords from overcharging their tenants and also for protection from sudden eviction, the Rent Control Act was hence modified.

As a breather for residents paying unreasonable property tax, the amounts were regulated in many states of India. Since property tax is one of the leading portions accounted in the income tax of a resident, regulating it was beneficial and essential for the common man. Another positive step was the initiative to computerize land records.

And in this way, slowly but surely, the real estate sector transformed into an organized sector.

IN TODAY'S WORLD...

The government is currently executing the 12th *Five Year Plan* for the year 2016-2017.

Today, India's industrial output depends heavily on infrastructure growth (about 26.7%). The Planning Commission has predicted a double increase in expenditure on infrastructure that would amount to approximately USD 1,025 Billion.

WHEN REAL ESTATE GOT WINGS!

In 2005, the government gave the approval for construction and development projects by introducing 100% foreign direct investment. Ever since this move, there has been no stopping the growth of this sector, although it did hit a few hurdles and a slow-down, which is but natural in this type of industry. The construction development sector in India has got FDI inflows of USD 24 billion from the beginning of the millennium up till the year 2015. It ranks 3rd out of 14 in direct, indirect as well as induced effects in all sectors of the economy.

Revised investor policies allow minimum-sized housing estates to be built with foreign capital ranging from a minimum of 10 hectares (25 acres) up to 40 hectares (100 acres).

The middle class man's qualms about the lack of affordable housing resonated and due to this the government took appropriate steps. Hence, in the year 2015, the new government announced reforms to further bring in foreign capital into the real estate sector.

The government also announced the mission 'Housing for All by 2022'. Under this Mission (Sardar Patel Urban Housing Mission), an expected 30 million houses will be constructed for low-income and economically-weaker sections of the society through Public-Private-Partnership (PPP) and subsidy on interest.

STATE OF RESIDENTIAL REAL ESTATE...

If we trace the promising endeavour of residential real estate, it begins at the dawn of the millennium. It is considered to have grown in four different phases – initial (2001-2005), high growth (2006-2008), slowdown (2009-2010), and finally consolidation (2011-2014).

At the end of the second phase, the housing shortage in India was estimated to be at 79 million units. The third phase saw the sky-high expectations of builders and investors crash due to the recession that took place globally. At the end of the fourth phase, the housing shortage was estimated to be at 75 million units. This indicated that irrespective of the growth, a shortfall continued to exist. This is majorly attributed to constant migration of populations to urban locations.

For directly uplifting that percent of the population below the poverty line, schemes such as Indira Aawaas Yojna, Two Million Housing Programme and Rajeev Gandhi Aawaas Yojna have contributed to 7% decrease in shortage numbers (currently, 53.8 million).

> ◆ Yet, investments in real estate in urban locations still flourish due to the constant demand-supply gap as well as because of the constantly increasing population.

The most popular investment destinations for NRIs have not changed over the last decade – Ahmedabad, Pune, Chennai, Goa, Delhi and Dehradun continue to rule, because the allure of the metropolitan cities is always present.

Currently, the metropolitan market that is performing the best in India is Bangalore in Karnataka. On the other hand, other main markets like Chennai, Delhi NCR and Gurgaon are facing low sales and year-on-year sales are recorded to have dropped to 50%.

TIER II, III CITIES – FUTURE OF INDIAN REAL ESTATE...

Tier II and Tier III cities that host populations of one million or less respectively, are hailed as *'The Future of Indian Real Estate'*. But why?

It is attributed to the saturation of metropolitans which bring in people to such cities.

More people, but lesser housing available – this gap was identified and major builders began organized investment to create real estate projects which were affordable due to the large availability of land. The investments were and are made consistently in an attempt to convert them into business havens.

> **Since 2005, Tier II cities Pune, DehraDun, Cochin, Pondicherry, Nagpur, Rajkot, among others benefitted from the *Jawaharlal Nehru National Urban Renewal Mission* (JNNURM) scheme which undertook modernisation of these particular cities.**

The biggest benefit of such cities is that the government actively involves itself in the region's development. It offers investment incentives as well as infrastructural aid. The creation of *Special Economic Zones (SEZs)* or *Free-Zones,* which have relaxed laws in order to encourage foreign investment, has truly pioneered the shining of Gujarat, Karnataka, Odisha and Maharashtra, among others.

Metro rail projects have been planned for Jaipur, Kochi, Pune, Chandigarh, Ahmedabad, Kanpur, Ludhiana, Bhopal, Indore, and Faridabad.

Tier III cities such as Nasik, Baroda, Madurai, Aligarh, Kochi, and Meerut, among others present an interesting situation for developers. In such locations, developers focus on affordable housing options for the industrial workforce. Interestingly, national developers do not perform that well as regional developers here and this may be because they understand the geography better than national players.

 **Overall, Ahmedabad, Bhubaneswar, Chandigarh, Coimbatore, Jaipur, Kochi, Indore, Nagpur, Vadodara, and Visakhapatnam have been listed as the top ten emerging cities of India.**

Coimbatore has become a hub for SMEs while Vishakhapatnam has become a hub for industries such as mining and heavy manufacturing. The city of Jaipur has been identified as a great service sector investment and Ahmedabad has been identified as a great manufacturing sector investment.

A 'SMART' TOMORROW

Pushing India into the league of world-class living is the Mission of building 100 'Smart City' projects.

The Mission has got a budget of ₹480 billion. Alongside this, the 'Atal Mission for Rejuvenation and Urban Transformation' (AMRUT) aimed at rejuvenating 500 cities has received a total funding of ₹500 billion from the Cabinet.

The Smart City Mission aims at converting a village or town-like region into an urban one, which is highly advanced in terms of overall infrastructure, sustainable real estate, communications, and market viability. In such cities, IT is the principal infrastructure.

Bhubaneshwar, Pune, Jaipur, Surat, Jabalpur, Solapur, Guwahati, and Ludhiana are among the first smart cities to receive funding and have started implementation. Bhubaneswar has recently launched a 'railway multi-modal hub', 'traffic signalisation project', and 'urban knowledge centre'. Similarly, Ahmedabad and New Delhi have launched 'smart learning in municipal schools', 'mini-sewerage treatment plants', 'smart LED streetlights', 'city surveillance' among others.

The opportunities for developers are great; so bigger and better projects which reverberate with global buyers are being planned.

THE CORPORATE STRATEGY

Corporate houses have corpus funds dedicated specially for the purpose of purchasing real estate which are undeniably important assets. The main purpose is to have these assets available to trade when the company requires liquidity. Real estate is encouraged as a diversification strategy in the investment portfolio for many companies.

Commercial real estate industry is skyrocketing but more recently, with the advent of MNCs, ownership of office space is no longer a necessity. Leasing is becoming more and more popular because of the convenience and lower cost of transactions.

Tier I city land prices have constantly escalated over the years. In earlier times, investing in land was regarded as both safe and sensible, regardless of how it was to be used, and would therefore produce capital gains far above the inflation rate. Many manufacturing and service industries acquired property completely unrelated to their area of expertise. From this, they generated property rent, collateral value, tax benefits from depreciated assets, and expected unrealized gains to absorb business risk.

Thus, commercial real estate in India, consisting of more than just IT parks and hospitality units has developed by ten times in terms of speed to meet various requirements of the growing commercial sector.

Mumbai, Bangalore, Hyderabad, and New Delhi are leaders in the arena. Every state of the country has a specific leader in commercial real estate, but overall, the best performing companies are 3C, Indiabulls Real Estate Ltd, DLF, and Ambuja, amongst others.

The diversity of realtors offering fresh solutions to prospects is encouraging local and global companies to establish their footing through leased offices.

TRANSPARENCY, POLICY AND VISION...

Identifying the main problem, that is, lack of transparency, in turn leads to lack of trust. Due to this, a series of steps were taken to fight this plague. Proactivity of the Indian government did bear fruit and due to this, measures were taken to increase the ease of doing business in the real estate sector. An increasing flow of FDI required further transparency and the government instructed developers to revamp their management and accounting.

One such landmark initiative was introduced in the Parliament in 2011 but was passed only in early 2016.

> The Real Estate (Regulation and Development) Bill is aimed at making it easier for developers and buyers to finalize deals. While this will impact the cost of apartments, it also hopes to encourage fair play in the sector.

Providing compensation to buyers in case of delays in delivering projects, will force builders to stick to due delivery dates. Also, the selling of houses only on 'carpet area' instead of including costs of common areas (like gardens, stairs, etc.) will ensure buyers to only pay for what they will really use.

Overall, registering projects and updating their progress will soon become transparent through this law and it is truly a path-breaking reform set to change the real estate sector of India.

Funding is always a question mark and developers are usually and almost always cash-strapped. In order to ease investments, the Securities and Exchange Board of India (SEBI) announced regulations which will govern Real Estate Investment Trusts (REITs) and Infrastructure Investment Trusts (InvITs).

> **Securing permission for construction was once a very lengthy process, especially for local builders. One exemplary effort to make this process faster and smoother was designed by the Government of Kerala. They launched 'Sanketham', an online software for a standardised procedure, less corruption, no bribery, and maximum transparency. Other states are expected to follow their lead.**

Focussing only on grants and investments are not enough though. The Ministry of Housing and Urban Poverty Alleviation (HUPA) fully understands that new construction and housing technologies must be discovered and tested, thus it invests in the same in association with Indian Institute of Technology, Kanpur.

THINGS LOOKING UP...
Special Economic Zones (SEZs) are emerging along with an addition to the real estate sector. There are townships being developed within SEZs with residential areas, markets, etc. These are called 'Special Residential Zones' and have got 100% FDI allowed as well.

The process of approvals has been consciously streamlined to ensure lesser delays and therefore smoother workings. Building layouts, ownership, environment clearances, structural planning, utilities – were both time-consuming and cumbersome. The delays often cause increase in costs which ultimately trickle down to the buyers. Hence, it was important to facilitate policy measures that streamlined approval processes (both at state as well as at national level), which helped in reducing the number of approvals required for real estate projects.

◆ { The spatial spreading of real estate and India's infrastructure is imperative. The development of peripheral towns has been largely led by the private sector.

In overview, a stable government steers steady growth and supports the development of infrastructure for the benefit of all. As India progresses into becoming one of the greatest economies globally, real estate will play its part and act as a major contributor.

REAL ESTATE INDUSTRY AS IT IS TODAY

Real estate is and will continue to play a part in driving the economic growth of the country, just as it has in the past. It is barely an understatement to say its valuation runs in "billions of dollars". The *sector is a proud* contributor of about 8.5% of the total GDP. Over the last decade, it has witnessed a *growth* rate of 30% despite the global economic uncertainty. This phenomenal growth is driven in parts by various factors like investments by NRIs, digital trends, upcoming government missions, and initiatives amongst other factors.

> **The Indian consumer has indeed provided the required vector to aid the growth of real estate industry in India. A sharp drive of consumerism has driven the real estate sector to a greater height.**

But ***what is consumerism***? It is a social and economic order "which encourages the buying of goods and services in greater amounts". The unprecedented amount of investment in all the Indian states is a by-product (or more) of consumerism. It can also be identified as a regulatory process in which standards are being brought into effect to benefit the consumer. In 1969, Indians had expressed concern over the quality of consumer goods and this concern led to the formation of the Consumer Protection Act, 1986. Lately, in a more globalized India, the media plays an important role in creating a lust for goods which are often, not guided by needs. Buyers in India are on the verge of losing their conscious ability to tell ***"What do I need?"*** apart from

"What do I want?". India is poised for a dramatic expansion of domestic consumption, making it one of the largest consumer markets in the world.

Consumerism can be held as the main cause for the Automobile Revolution in India. The real estate sector also experienced a similar revolution when a multitude of global brands entered the country. This was followed by a boom in real estate advertising which in turn was followed by rapid infrastructural growth. Currently, consumerism in India, which is building on 300 million middle-class households is supported by current GDP growth in the region of 9%.

An increase in disposable income along with the tremendous exposure of Western culture has led to the boom of *luxury real estate market*. It comprises of 10% of the total residential market and is also expected to grow further and multiply 2.5 times its current size in the upcoming five years. New concepts, innovations in home design, technology, home automation, and eco-friendliness along with other global trends are exploding in this sector! Dedicated to the seasoned consumer, ideally in urban markets, properties range from INR 1.5 crore and can scale up to INR 25 crore. The growth of this sector is directly proportional to the growth of the overall real estate market.

According to statistics, the number of 'Super Rich' in India will parallel China's current levels in a decade. Who would have thought? Aspirations run higher each day and an estimated 9000 luxury homes are being planned across major Indian cities currently.

It is barely debatable that the *escalation of NRI Population* is contributing to the same. Who are NRIs anyway? A non-resident Indian (NRI) is a citizen of India holding an Indian passport, who has temporarily immigrated to another country (for six months or more) for education, work, residence, or any other purpose. India boasts of having the largest diaspora population in the world. As of 2015, 17 million Indians are living abroad.

Simple transaction rules encourage more purchases. The transaction of property for an NRI falls under the Foreign Exchange Management Act (FEMA). Also, monetary transactions are made through normal banking channels in INR.

> **According to the norms of the RBI, a maximum of 80% of the value of the property can be funded by a financial institution while the rest has to come from the NRI's personal resources.**

Only graduate NRIs are open to availing home loans in India.

For these people, real estate is a lucrative investment option as the Rupee falls against international currencies. Although the prices of property have increased greatly over the last seven years, it is only a marginal increase for those living abroad. *Why do they impact on Real Estate?* Irrespective of the market status ('hot or not'), NRIs are always on the lookout for residential and sometimes commercial investments back home. There is no restriction on the number of properties they can buy, however, they cannot purchase farm houses, plantation property or agricultural land. Developers focus a lot of energy on attracting investments from NRIs. Many, like the Hiranandani Group, have devoted architects and designed townships especially with NRIs in mind. On an average, transactions worth 3 crores or more are required to gain great ROI. The rental income from commercial property makes it an increasingly preferred choice of investment.

In contrast to luxury, India is also tackling some issues at its foundation. India is all set to become the most populous nation in the world in the upcoming decade. Obviously, this will lead to a large vacuum in the housing sector. The current condition of housing in India is very concerning as India is short of about six crore houses. Currently, the housing sector of real estate ropes in around USD 120 billion. Central and State governments are only spending USD 5 billion per annum (3%) of investments in the sector. Uneven distribution of the housing development in rural areas is another cause of concern. Understanding that the economically-weak sections of the society will suffer due to this, the *'Housing for All by 2022'* initiative was launched by the government. This move is definitive in timeline as well as in scope. But is it *a Mission or just a Manifesto?*

To elaborate, the encouraging *vision of the government* is all set to tackle the plague of the real estate sector and bring in the following. It has raised the bar for many troublesome aspects of the sector.

> *Higher Investments*: **Roping in USD 260 billion worth of investments annually until 2022 which must grow at 13% CAGR.**
>
> *Faster Approvals:* **A project less than 50,000 square meters will not require any environmental clearance.**
>
> *Self-Certification*: **Qualified architects can self-certify projects to ensure regulations are being followed.**
>
> *Leveraging Technology*: **Modern, innovative green technologies, building material, and environment-friendly layouts after coordinating with energy efficiency agencies to combat climate change.**

The Mission targets that *110 million dwelling LIG units* (Low Income Group units) will have to be built according to a conservative estimate. 'Affordable homes' are the need of the hour – truly a herculean task for the government. The capital requirements for the fulfilment is expected to be about $2 trillion. The revocation of unfavourable policies like the Urban Land Ceiling Act and FSI ceiling policies will increase the supply of land to the affordable housing segment leading to higher supply at lower cost, which will benefit the industry. Public housing projects cannot meet this demand alone; it must be with support from the private sector. As per the plan, 30 lakh houses need to be built every year till 2022 to meet the target.

Among other measures, the government is also set to introduce global standards for building and construction process, reduced interest rates, and the introduction of REITs and FDI in real estate.

Also, a part of this initiative is the **Slum Rehabilitation Programme,** through which the government will try to help promote affordable housing for the weaker section through credit-linked subsidy. Private developers will play an active role in developing the land and constructing houses. What is the dimension of the task? An estimated two crore houses must be built to satiate immediate needs. These numbers have been assessed through identification of intended beneficiaries from the Aadhar card number and Jan Dhan Yojana account numbers.

Early 2014-2015 saw some great pro-reformation steps which rekindled hope for growth in the real estate sector. A landmark initiative, **Real Estate Investment Trusts (REITs)** is expected to be greatly beneficial for the sector as it attempts to introduce a new internationally-acclaimed investment structure in India. These Trusts are aimed at protecting the consumers' interests. For a REIT to be feasible, the Ministry of Finance has also made amendments to the tax regime. Private Equity funds that were planning to launch their own REITs cannot do the same as they are threatened by how the MAT (Minimum Alternate Tax) might make them unviable. Unfortunately, the foreign investments in assets and applicability of MAT have struck this regime as a drawback. But the government continues to take steps to create a conducive, investor-friendly environment at REITs. They might also scrap 'stamp duty' during the transfer of properties by firms and private individuals to REITs.

 **Another Act that has established itself in the real estate sector which is definitely very encouraging is the *Right to Fair Compensation and Transparency in Land Acquisition,***

 *Rehabilitation and Resettlement Act (LARR)* which came into effect in early 2014 before which it was guided by an archaic law, the Land Acquisition Act of 1894. LARR makes the process of acquiring land by the State governments for their use, control, and also for public sector undertakings or other "public purposes" easier.

Initially introduced in the Parliament in 2011 but passed in early 2016, *the Real Estate (Regulation and Development) Bill* is dedicated to making the process of finalizing deals between buyers and developers easier.

It may increase the cost of apartments in general but is aimed at encouraging fair play in this sector. It recommends establishing *'State Real Estate Regulatory Authorities'* which will address grievances against errant builders. It extends to residential as well as commercial real estate purchases. Any projects of more than 500 sq. m. up to eight apartment towers are required to be registered with the RERA. The Bill also ensures that prices are quoted on carpet area, not on super area. Developers will face penalties if they deviate the building plans without gaining the consent of 66% of the buyers. Builders are now required to share the project layout and plan, land title status, subcontractors involved, and schedule for completion with the buyers.

A delay penalty of the same interest as the EMI being paid by the buyer to the bank will be levied if the structures are not completed on time. Also, buyers can demand after-sales service from the developer within one year of possession.

Digital disruption is everywhere so how can we expect real estate to be left out? Technological alternatives to time-taking processes are saving time and sending across information in a jiffy. Due to the expansion of real estate online, buyers today are now better informed than ever before!

> The process of *acquiring loans* and the processing time for loans for home buyers/developers has turned around due to the online approach of financial institutions. Local brokers are going out of business due to the sector's introductory shift to the digital platform!

The property listing aggregators (websites like Magicbricks, Housing.com, and 99Acres.com) entered the market and offered a plethora of purchase options. Buyers take minutes to decide from these elaborate databases according to relevant criteria (location, area, prices, amenities, etc.). Brokerages have plummeted. Also, **online 'house hunting'** has changed renting and selling from the perspective of a property owner.

Not long ago, it was unimaginable to have Approved Plans made available online by the Municipal corporations. Now, Title Records, an updated information base regarding acts and by-laws as well as websites like MoEF and CZMA greatly contribute to average investors' knowledge. Today, we can view rates for Registration of built property and compare costs provided by developers. Online portfolios are more accessible. Last but not the least, data analytics quantify the information and add value and insight to it.

Be it building, marketing or loans, Indian real estate sector is fiercely going digital in the next decade!

CHAPTER 2

TYPES OF REAL ESTATE INVESTMENTS

"Use money to produce profit" – it's as simple as that. Does this definition of investment sound a bit too crude? Basic? If the answer is yes, then you're right, the phrase is from the year 1610. The principal motivation behind investments has remained the same till today. We invest as we expect a benefit in return. Through investments, we give a new shape and form to our capital.

The first few big investments most Indians make are small amounts of gold, a vehicle or a car and ultimately a house. The essentials of a stable life *'Roti, Kapda aur Makaan'* (Food, Clothes and House), which was also the slogan for Indian socialism, remains the focus of one section. Yet, there are a few of those who have secured the essentials and aspire for bigger and better.

For most of us, buying a house is a long process where there is no room for error! It is one of the most significant purchase decisions of an Indian household. We only undertake this journey when we are sure that we have the resources (which includes money) as well as time to follow up and ensure the purchase goes through smoothly. Simply choosing a home can be an ordeal for first-time buyers. They start hunting with the simple dream of having a beautiful and secure home that meets the spatial and emotional requirements of all family members. Depending on the fact if the house is already constructed or under construction, purchasing and registering the dream house in the right name is another long-winded process. But buyers with the right vigour swim across the challenges such as exorbitant prices, unfavourable home loans, low interest rates, lack of capital, etc.

THE RESIDENTIAL REAL ESTATE SECTOR OF INDIA

The residential real estate sector is the largest contributor to the real estate sector in India.

 **The urban landscape turned around in a matter of few years. Experts suggest that it has grown in four phases – initial (2001-2005), high growth (2006-2008), slowdown (2009-2010) and finally consolidation (2011-2014).**

It began with the construction of G+3 towers which have now increased up to G+24; G+60 is now not a far-fetched dream for some developers. One of the driving factors for swift urbanisation is the increasing growth of the Indian population and constant migration from rural and suburban towns to the cities. This necessitates a constant demand-supply gap which the industry works hard to meet. Yet, there is a shortfall.

As of 2015, the shortage of houses in urban India was 18.8 million houses. Several initiatives have been taken to uplift the population residing below the poverty line –Two Million Housing Programme, Rajeev Gandhi Aawaas Yojna – have currently contributed to 7% decrease in shortage in accommodation for this section of the society.

The plethora of options for residential real estate available can be classified as follows:

VILLA/BUNGALOW/ROW HOUSES

Independent residential plots are preferred for those who seek openness, exclusivity, comfort and luxury. These attributes make them immediately expensive but are also in very high demand. The house can be designed as per the buyer's requirements in such a case. If it is not built on time, heavy penalties are charged. But, even though there is vast personal space, residential plots often face zoning and encroachment issues.

CONDOMINIUMS

 **Increasingly, the homes designed for nuclear families are most desired in the market and are available at a variety of price points to suit different classes of prospective buyers.**

More and more working couples with busy schedules are the major buyers of 'gated community' properties (better known as condominiums) that consist of facilities like gardens, gyms, grocery stores, shopping complexes or malls at their doorsteps. But of course, high maintenance costs and limits to extend the house for future needs inhibit many buyers.

STUDIO APARTMENTS

Studio apartments are fast gaining popularity among bachelors, small families and professionals. These properties are comparatively economical and are often available on low EMI payments. Such a real estate option is a great choice for those looking for passive income by renting their properties out.

SERVICE APARTMENTS

Service apartments are also gaining popularity. They can be small or large with different kinds of facilities. They can be more spacious than a hotel room with a kitchen, bathroom and also other facilities like telephone, fax and an internet connection. Housekeeping staff and concierge services make service apartments a cheaper alternative compared to hotels. Even though owners can barely stay at their properties, if they are well-situated, returns can be anywhere around 9-14% through occupancy throughout the year. Usually, the developer maintains the property professionally and the owner need not worry about it.

PAYMENT PLANS – WHICH ONE SHOULD YOU CHOOSE?

In a Construction-Linked Plan (CLP), the developer receives instalments which the bank sends on your behalf at specific construction milestones. You only start repaying the loan after you get the property i.e. the first EMI starts after you gain possession. CLP is tricky because the buyer pays rent and pre-EMI during the construction period of the loan. The main drawback – no transparency or accountability on how developers utilize their instalments. There is also no regulatory body to report to.

In a Down Payment Plan (DPP), the buyer has to pay 10% of the cost of the house as the booking amount. Once booked, about 80% has to be paid within 30 days. In DPPs, the builder usually settles for 10-12% lesser than the cost of the property. The main issue is of the risk that the construction might not complete on time, or that it will wrap up midway.

Next is the Possession-Linked Plan. This is a combination of the above-stated options. The buyer pays 1/3rd of the price while booking; 1/3rd at specific milestones and the rest when they get possession. No risks of delayed construction and there's lesser cash in question. Of course, it comes with the disadvantage of a 'premium fee' which is applied on the standard rate (usually 10-15%). Don't forget to negotiate!

Today, everyone booking in the residential real estate segment opts for the possession-linked plan. The buyer's risk is limited to the initial investment (20-25%) which buyers pay to book apartments. This plan was devised by builders to combat the delays in possession which can easily extend from 2 to 5 years. It is favoured against the construction-linked plan.

Registering projects (possession-linked plans) and updating their progress will see a new level of transparency through the Real Estate (Regulation and Development) Act, which is a working law since May 1st, 2016.

TOP REALTORS

The repatriation of HNIs and also Non-Resident Indians has encouraged real estate developers to aim bigger. Also, holiday homes in Goa and Dehradun still remain a popular concept.

The biggest projects where NRIs invested the most were undertaken in Mumbai by Hiranandani Developers, Indiabulls Real Estate, Oberoi Realty; in Bangalore by Puravankara, Brigade Group; in Delhi NCR by 3C, DLF, Amrapali Group, Jaypee Group; in Kolkata by Forum Projects, Ideal Group, Merlin Group, among others.

> Some big realtors like Godrej Properties Ltd have adopted the strategy of partnering with local construction firms or operators to provide varied offerings in residential property all over the country.

SO WHICH RESIDENTIAL PROPERTY DO YOU WANT TO INVEST IN?

A number of options have been laid out above. While residential real estate investments do not particularly 'mature' like equity investments, the return on investment for these are often around 3-5% per annum.

A residential property appreciates sharply. Also, if they are located close to prime spots such as malls, schools or other such helpful public facilities, there is never a dearth of tenants lining up outside who would like to rent it. Once on rent, maintenance also becomes their responsibility.

 **Another stark positive is that loans are readily available in case you would like to make a purchase. In most cases, up to 70% of the total property cost is available by external sources like banks.**

Residential real estate is also very easy to sell in comparison with its counterparts but buyers should still choose wisely!

COMMERCIAL REAL ESTATE SECTOR IN INDIA

INDIA TODAY MEANS BUSINESS!

The simultaneous and steady boom of retail chains, entertainment and hospitality sector (resorts, malls, etc.) alongside a fast-developing information technology and service sector have put India on the international map for *commercial real estate investment* opportunities.

 A huge jump in commercial investment commitments took place during the 'Make in India' week in Mumbai, 2015 – Rs. 15.2 trillion across various states of India.

It drove the leasing activity in the manufacturing sector in 2016 bringing in Samsung and Honeywell in Gurgaon, Oppo in Noida, Renault-Nissan and Ford in Mumbai, among others.

The increase in business opportunities in metropolitan cities is backed by the labour force which has migrated from rural areas. This has ensured projects, especially commercial housing spaces which are developing at three-fold speed compared to the previous decades.

DEMAND FOR COMMERCIAL WORK SPACES

Not surprising that the demand for office and commercial work spaces has contributed to Bangalore being the top commercial real estate investment destination of the country. This technology-rich city harbours IT parks, numerous luxury hospitality as well as retail properties and boasts a diversity of realtors who are offering out-of-the-box solutions to prospects. Multinationals who think of expansion into India almost involuntarily think Bangalore, and then New Delhi and Mumbai. Hyderabad has been selected as Apple's first tech development centre outside the USA ever since the government eased FDI rules for single brand retailing and relaxed the procurement conditions for technology companies.

TOP COMMERCIAL REALTORS

Hiranandani Developers are leaders in commercial spaces in Mumbai, K Raheja Constructions, Indiabulls Real Estate; in Bangalore, Ascendas, Brigade Group and Bagmane Developers are current leaders.

In Delhi, 3C, ASF Infrastructure, DLF while in Kolkata, Ambuja Neotia, DLF and Srijan Group are leaders in the field.

CONFUSED ABOUT THE RETURNS ON COMMERCIAL INVESTMENTS VS. RESIDENTIAL INVESTMENTS?

It's simple, even though the prices of commercial properties do not appreciate as fast as residential properties, the returns on commercial are GREAT!

Investors looking at commercial properties will forego a very high transaction cost; but needless to say, the returns are well worth it. The drawback is that banks do not offer loans for the purchase of commercial properties unless they are complete. But, the rental returns range from 7-13% per annum. However, it may require up to eight years to obtain such high returns.

Commercial buildings have a number of owners and can host properties as small as 500 sq. ft. Sometimes, builders have schemes where they give 12% interest on the money deposited for a project which gives ownership of small units of 500 sq. ft. to individual customers.

In this case, builders take money and return the same money to you in instalments as interest. If you ask them for a discount on the projected construction, the builders will take money from you and handover a proportionate discount. In some cases, the builder gives 12% interest on deposits for construction to customers who give a lump sum money, then it costs them about 18% interest on that amount.

This can be beneficial – the money is securely placed away for a long period of time and one gets a steady return over several years. Imagine the premises you have purchased remain vacant for some reason. The maintenance cost from your pocket can be very high – almost Rs. 20 per sq. ft. In case the builders take on the maintenance of the premises, the owner and tenant should get an agreement signed.

 **The location of the commercial property is a big factor while selecting where to invest. If it is far from the industrial heart and hub of the area, then it may be difficult to charge a higher rent.**

But, there is a large amount of physical control over commercial properties – such as picking and choosing rental clients/tenants, negotiation over rent, etc. Large floor areas are preferred by companies. Lease and agreements are generally renewed after every 3 years. The escalation clause states a 15% increment. The lessee may also ask for a tenancy period of 9 years.

Yet, rental yields are completely dependent on tenants as when buying commercial space/s, you also indirectly buy an 'income stream' from potential tenants. So choosing a right tenant is an undertaking of great risk. At times, even reputed brands may default on monthly payments, or companies may go broke and wrap up their operations – in such a case, there is little the property owner can do, except for legally filing a case against them.

RETAIL REAL ESTATE SECTOR

Organized retail sector of India is estimated to grow up to 560 crores by the end of 2016. Tier-1 and Tier-2 cities of Mumbai, NCR Delhi, Chennai, Kolkata, Bangalore, Pune, and Hyderabad account for over 70 percent of the entire country's total retail stock! According to a JLL report, they are the key centres of *retail real estate investment* in India. A good, stable economy and high disposable income drives retail-based growth. Although expanding quickly, all of the retail space in India is only 1/4th of the retail space available throughout China.

IT'S A MALL, MALL WORLD!

A younger and more vibrant India welcomes their swiftly expanding national and international retail options. Earlier, luxury retail had a limited presence in the top 5 cities of the country. However, it is not the case anymore. Primarily, the steady demand from fashion, food & beverages sector helped keep rents stable in many cities.

The more developed the infrastructure of a city is, retail outlets will flourish there.

In this fast-moving world of retail and leisure, people are now turning to solutions delivered for higher performance or 'retail intelligence' advisors. These advisors are ideal as they manage local as well as international retail space commitments and have a wide exposure to the market.

CHALLENGES OF OCCUPANCY

In 2011-13, economic activity slowed down and huge chunks of retail mall space remained vacant. What could cause such vacancies in Indian cities compared to other ASEAN cities? The JLL report claims it is due to a large number of poor to average grade malls – whose superior counterparts created a demand polarization.

From this, an underlying trend can be fathomed. The masses lean towards superior quality malls with better retail and entertainment facilities; their average standard of entertainment, expectation and in turn, standard of living has risen. Realtors attempt to create a wholesome 'all-in-one' mall by accommodating all services under one roof and thereby increasing the average size of a mall in India.

Oddly, Delhi, Mumbai and Pune are facing very large vacancies. Each of these cities witnessed development of retail space inventory over the last five years – due to an influx of investment in the retail sector and the development of infrastructure which further pushed retail growth.

SALE MODEL OR LEASE MODEL?

Ownership is an important factor that influences vacancy rates of malls. According to the JLL Report, malls that use the Sale Model are likely to have a higher vacancy rate. This could be because they lack proper management, zoning and tenant mix. The Lease Model performs drastically better. 60% of Indian malls operate using this method. It has become popular with developers who can execute a better quality mall with this Model.

MORE URBAN, MORE WESTERN

A surge of international retail chains into the country ensured good absorption of retail spaces in cities like Chennai, Pune, Delhi, Bangalore and Mumbai. The 'zations' driving this forward are Urbanization and Westernization. These two are the main drivers for change in the character of the consumers, maturing markets and new retail opportunities.

SO, WHAT MAKES A SUCCESSFUL MALL?

 **Why are some projects failing? Is it the location, mall management, supply benchmarking or simply the parking? The management must chalk out an intelligent, effective marketing plan for all year-round. Malls must undertake planning and positioning initiatives from the beginning.**

An increasing demand for quality mall space has forced many retailers to pay a 'premium lease' in a superior performing mall. The shopping mall industry needs to adopt a structured approach for planning and execution/opening of the malls.

A good tenant mix will ensure both optimum and maximum utilization of space. During 2006-07, several developers rushed to make malls without paying adequate attention to design and design mix. Although the land was purchased in prime areas at high costs, the footfall was simply not enough. A well-layed out mall will definitely experience repeated footfall.

E-commerce giants are a constant threat to the mall industry. To combat stiff competition from them, mall management has to provide customers with new experiences. Going to the mall has to entertain and engage consumers or why would they choose to leave home and visit when they can simply shop with the click of a button?

HOW CAN YOU INVEST IN RETAIL REAL ESTATE?

Retail can be slow at times but yet it offers one of the highest yields – from 10 to 15%. Buying retail space is very different from other real estate. The dynamics are different.

Before investing, search for the 'catchment area' of the mall, i.e. residences that house populations above 5 lakhs in the vicinity. This method works for towns and suburban areas as well.

A popular technique is buying multiple shops within a mall. These shops should be adjacent to one another so that they can fit large format requirements also when required. But of course, assess the mall's administration before you create a long term plan with them. In general, developers have reduced selling space in malls to individual investors since it is difficult to manage.

An upcoming concept is - creating projects with homes, a mall, office space and even a hotel. This is known as 'mixed use'. A variety of risks can be averted through this format since residential and office spaces have a captive demand. Although it is innovative, currently this model is not performing well in India. Dedicated properties are better.

 Overall, retail investments are a great option for HNIs looking to spend a few crores (anywhere ranging from 2-25 crores) with expected returns of about 11%.

INDUSTRIAL REAL ESTATE SECTOR IN INDIA

Industrial real estate properties have to host machinery that fits the needs of the client and has to be highly customized to the industry it wants to cater to. It can range from milk production units to being a warehouse for fertilizers to producing iron ore to welding logos for a luxury car brand... the possibilities are endless.

CATEGORIES OF INDUSTRIAL REAL ESTATE

Let's start from the smaller units which provide a certain amount of flexibility with the interiors, better known as *'flex warehouses'*. Such buildings can be two-storeys and consist of go-down and office space conveniently. Start-ups, labs, etc. are readily available tenants for these places.

Moving on to a larger space used for assembling products, better known as *'light assembly'* real estate. Product assembling equipment, space to store raw materials and products, and also office quarters are available in such properties.

 **The biggest manufacturing, rather *'heavy manufacturing'* properties are enormous by design – anywhere between 40 thousand to one million sq. ft. They constitute very specific machinery which is ordered as per the tenants' needs.**

Obviously, if a new tenant joins, the place has to be re-done from scratch to suit their industrial requirements.

Also available are warehouses of different sizes which are specifically designed to support distribution of products. They are located in places close to interstate highways or major road links. Number of big trucks are in and out of the area multiple times a day depending on the type of distribution. Heavy manufacturing properties also often acquire these warehouses to store products.

WHY DOESN'T THE AVERAGE MAN THINK OF INVESTING IN INDUSTRIAL REAL ESTATE?

There are so many inhibiting factors – initial investment costs, the size and the eventual risks of vacancy.

Such properties have to be either enormous or large so as to find the right tenant/client. In order to acquire such an asset, a buyer always has to borrow from banks.

 **Banks are cautious about industrial investments and interest rates are higher than other property investments. They ask for up to 20-30% in deposits.**

Market situation directly affects industrial properties. In times of low economic growth or recession, suppose a company closes down and leaves the property empty, the owner faces no rent for an extended period. Searching for a suitable tenant in such times is difficult.

Considering how swiftly technology is changing these days, all the machinery the buyer invests in is subject to obsolescence.

WHY SHOULD YOU CONSIDER INDUSTRIAL REAL ESTATE?

The yields per annum! A very favourable rent can offer up to 8%. An average lease runs from 4-5 years. Security is guaranteed since sometimes long-term leases can run up to 10 years, with fixed yearly

41

increments in price. Industrial leases are inclusive of maintenance and repair and also insurance which the owner has to pay in usual cases.

BUY, LEASE OR DO BOTH?

 **Some savvy investors usually both own as well as lease industrial properties in different locations for stability. The flexible choices of occupying, expanding and contracting help generate more income.**

GET EXPERT HELP!

Institutions often turn to industrial real estate professionals who have in-depth knowledge and expertise across various fields like warehouse, manufacturing and distribution. They can help with analysing the cost of having your property occupied, whether the distribution technology is up to date, whether flexibility can be found with tenants, etc. Guidance during leasing, buying, developing, renovating, and also selling is available from them.

Uttar Pradesh, Gujarat, Punjab and Maharashtra have become industrial hubs.

 **Currently, Tier I cities' industrial property is reaching a point of saturation. Companies are constantly looking to have bases beyond the city. Acquiring industrial property in towns and suburban regions can be an insightful long term investment.**

HYBRID REAL ESTATE SECTOR

Investors purchase fixer-upper real estate properties at a low cost and then turn them upside down within weeks to sell them at a much higher cost. This is what we call as "Flipping" properties. While such stories are not very common, a lot of people throughout the world do it and earn handsome returns within a short span of time. And the classic method of "Buy and Hold" is something that needs no introduction.

While both "Flipping" and "Buy and Hold" strategies are great and carry great potential, people generally choose one of the two to get best returns on their investment. Hybrid real estate investing is a method that provides the investors with the benefits from "Flipping" as well as "Buy and Hold" strategies. This type of investing is generally recommended for experienced investors as it requires a keen eye in selecting properties and knowledge about the market conditions to ensure maximum profits.

The first step of investing in a hybrid real estate property is selecting a property that needs help, especially the one that needs cosmetic help like carpet, paint, countertops, etc.

 **The property should not be available at very steep discounts as these properties often need a major amount of repairs. Such properties are often ideal for professional flippers.**

As a hybrid real estate investor, a property which comes at 70%-80% after repair cost can be a great choice.

After buying one such property, the next step is to get the cosmetic job done to make sure that it is in a rentable condition. Again, as a hybrid investor it is not necessary to make sure that the property is the best one in the local market as this is not the time to sell this property. Avoid very expensive remodeling and just ensure that it is in a good rentable condition.

Once the property is modified, rent it out to start earning rental income. It is important to understand that the real estate market works in cycles. Every crest is followed by a trough and vice versa. As Warren Buffet always mentions, "Buy when others are selling and sell when others are buying". As a hybrid investor, it is important to understand the market condition to make this strategy work and provide handsome returns.

And when the market is at its peak and people are buying, it is time to sell this property at the best possible rate and then invest this money again in a property that needs cosmetic help. However, the investor should avoid buying when the markets are at peak. Wait for the rates to come down, reinvest the money in another property and then continue this cycle all over again.

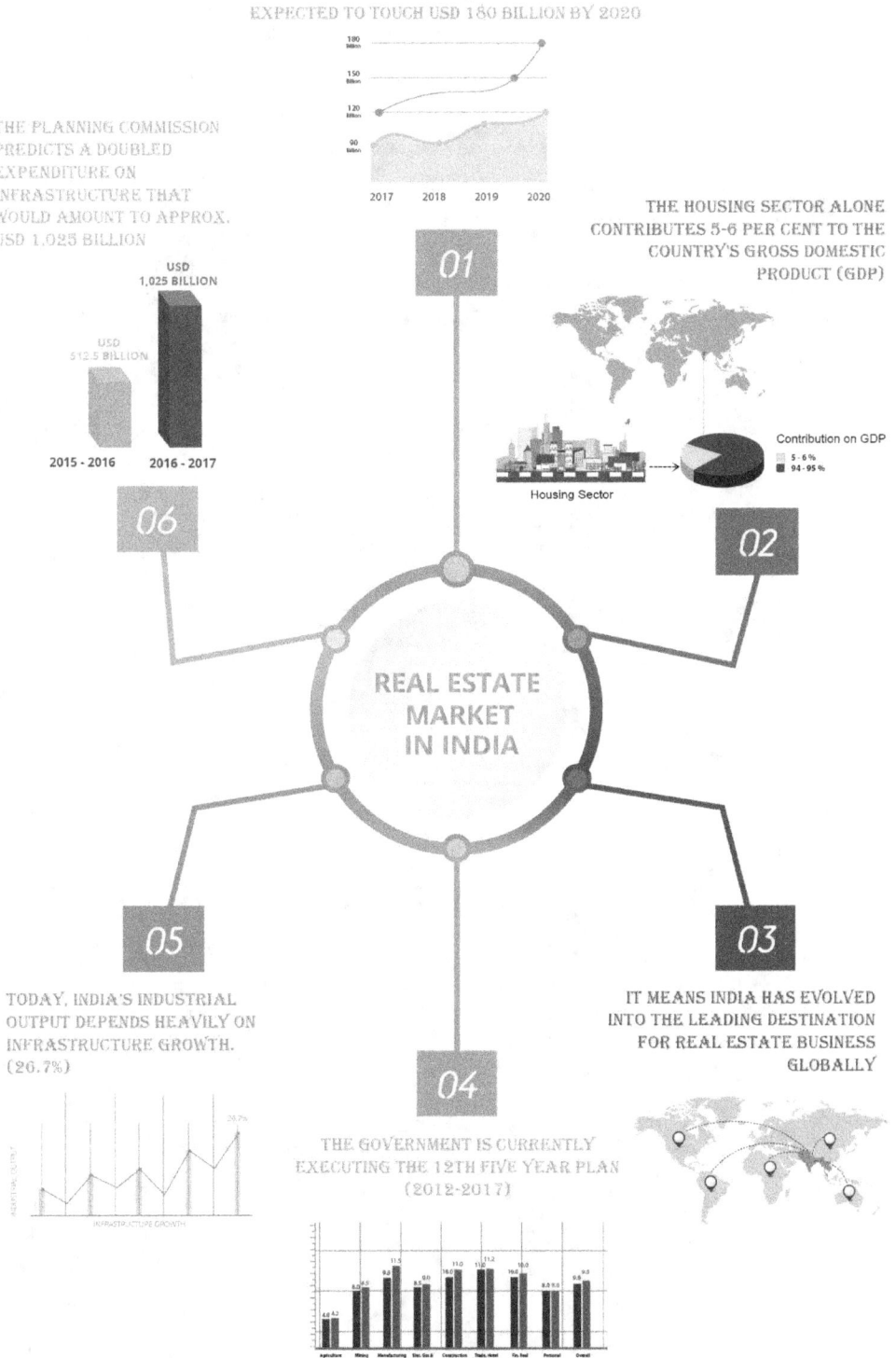

THE INDIAN REAL ESTATE MARKET IS
EXPECTED TO TOUCH USD 180 BILLION BY 2020

THE PLANNING COMMISSION
PREDICTS A DOUBLED
EXPENDITURE ON
INFRASTRUCTURE THAT
WOULD AMOUNT TO APPROX.
USD 1,025 BILLION

THE HOUSING SECTOR ALONE
CONTRIBUTES 5-6 PER CENT TO THE
COUNTRY'S GROSS DOMESTIC
PRODUCT (GDP)

USD
1,025 BILLION

USD
512.5 BILLION

2015 - 2016   2016 - 2017

Contribution on GDP
5 - 6 %
94 - 95 %

Housing Sector

REAL ESTATE
MARKET
IN INDIA

01

02

03

04

05

06

TODAY, INDIA'S INDUSTRIAL
OUTPUT DEPENDS HEAVILY ON
INFRASTRUCTURE GROWTH.
(26.7%)

IT MEANS INDIA HAS EVOLVED
INTO THE LEADING DESTINATION
FOR REAL ESTATE BUSINESS
GLOBALLY

THE GOVERNMENT IS CURRENTLY
EXECUTING THE 12TH FIVE YEAR PLAN
(2012-2017)

Tier II and Tier III cities that host populations of 1 million or less respectively, are hailed as 'The Future of Indian Real Estate'

Since 2005, Tier II cities Pune, Dehra Dun, Cochin, Pondicherry, Nagpur, Rajkot, among others, benefitted from the Jawaharlal Nehru National Urban Renewal Mission (JNNURM) scheme which undertook modernisation of these cities

01

02

Metro rail projects have been planned for Jaipur, Kochi, Pune, Chandigarh, Ahmedabad, Kanpur, Ludhiana, Bhopal, Indore, and Faridabad

03

Tier III cities such as Nasik, Baroda, Madurai, Aligarh, Kochi, Meerut, among others, represent an interesting situation for developers

04

TIER II, III CITIES – FUTURE OF INDIAN REAL ESTATE...

In such locations, developers focus on affordable housing options for industrial work forces

05

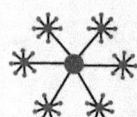

Overall, Ahmedabad, Bhubaneswar, Chandigarh, Coimbatore, Jaipur, Kochi, Indore, Nagpur, Vadodara and Visakhapatnam have been listed as the top ten emerging cities of India

06

07

Coimbatore has become a hub for SMEs while Vishakhapatnam has become a hub for industries such as mining, heavy manufacturing. Jaipur has been identified as a great service sector investment and Ahmedabad has been identified as a great manufacturing sector investment

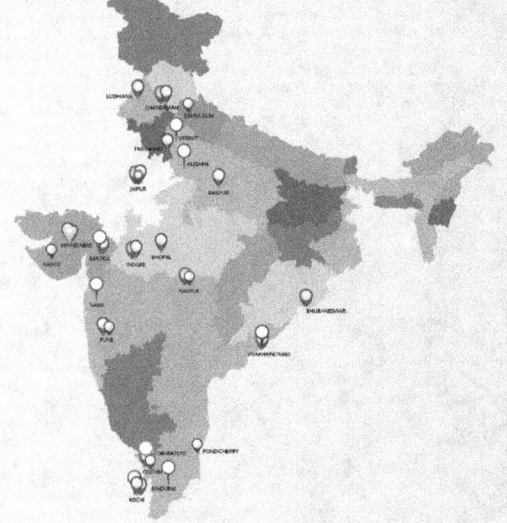

Tier II cities benefitted from the JNNURM scheme

Metro rail projects have been planned for these cities

Tier III cities represent an interesting situation for developers, Developers focus on affordable housing options for industrial work forces

Emerging cities of India

A hub for SMEs

A hub for industries such as mining, heavy manufacturing

Service sector investment

Manufacturing sector investment

TIER I CITY LAND PRICES HAVE CONSTANTLY ESCALATEDOVER THE YEARS

SAFE AND SENSIBLE INVESTMENT

Investing in land was regarded as both safe and sensible regardless of how it was to be used,would produce capital gains far above the inflation rate

UNRELATED PROPERTY

Many manufacturing and service industries acquired property completely unrelated to their area of expertise. From this they generated property rent, collateral value, tax benefits from depreciated assets, and expecting unrealized gains to absorb business risk

OPTION **01**

OPTION **02**

TIER I CITY LAND PRICES HAVE CONSTANTLY ESCALATED OVER THE YEARS

OPTION **03**

OPTION **04**

DEVELOPED AT 10 TIMES THE SPEED

Thus, commercial real estate in India consisting of more than just IT parks and hospitality units, has developed in ten times the speed to meet the various requirements of the growing commercial sector

LEADERS IN THE ARENA

Mumbai, Bangalore, Hyderabad and New Delhi are leaders in the arena. Every state of the country has a specific leader in commercial real estate, but overall the best performing companies are 3C, Indiabulls Real Estate Ltd, DLF, Ambuja, amongst others

01 VILLA/BUNGALOW/ ROW HOUSES

Independent residential plots are preferred for those who seek openness, exclusivity, comfort and luxury

02 CONDOMINIUMS

Increasingly, the homes designed for nuclear families are most desired in the market and are available at a variety of price points to suit different classes of prospective buyers

THE RESIDENTIAL REAL ESTATE SECTOR OF INDIA

SERVICE APARTMENTS 04

Studio apartments are fast gaining popularity among the bachelors, small families and professionals. These properties are comparatively economical and are often available on low EMI payments

STUDIO APARTMENTS 03

Service apartments are also gaining popularity. They can be small or large with different kinds of facilities, it can be more spacious than a hotel room with a kitchen, bathroom, and also other facilities like telephone, fax and an internet connection

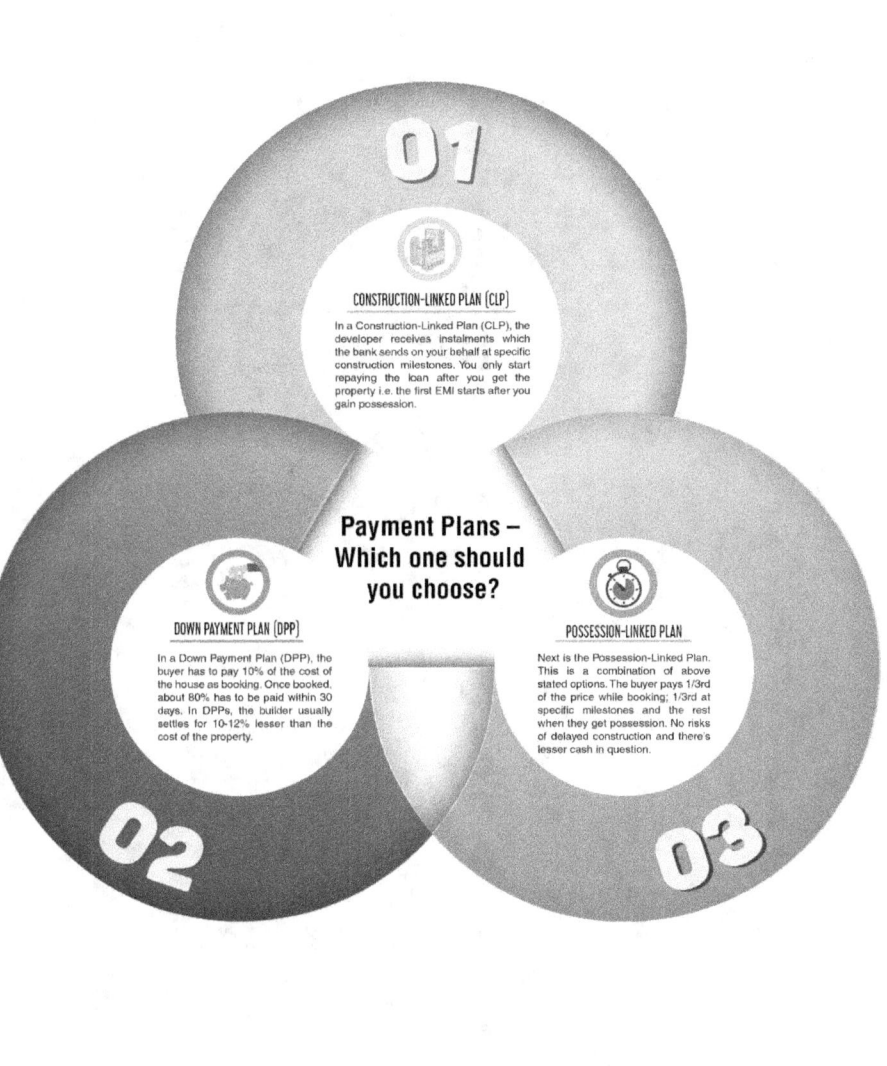

01

CONSTRUCTION-LINKED PLAN (CLP)

In a Construction-Linked Plan (CLP), the developer receives instalments which the bank sends on your behalf at specific construction milestones. You only start repaying the loan after you get the property i.e. the first EMI starts after you gain possession.

Payment Plans – Which one should you choose?

DOWN PAYMENT PLAN (DPP)

In a Down Payment Plan (DPP), the buyer has to pay 10% of the cost of the house as booking. Once booked, about 80% has to be paid within 30 days. In DPPs, the builder usually settles for 10-12% lesser than the cost of the property.

02

POSSESSION-LINKED PLAN

Next is the Possession-Linked Plan. This is a combination of above stated options. The buyer pays 1/3rd of the price while booking; 1/3rd at specific milestones and the rest when they get possession. No risks of delayed construction and there's lesser cash in question.

03

CONFUSED ABOUT THE RETURNS ON COMMERCIAL INVESTMENTS VS. RESIDENTIAL INVESTMENTS?

OWNERSHIP OF SMALL UNITS

Commercial buildings have a number of owners and can host properties as small as 500 sq. ft. Sometimes, builders have schemes where they give 12% interest on the money deposited for a project which gives ownership of small units of 500 sq. ft. to individual customers

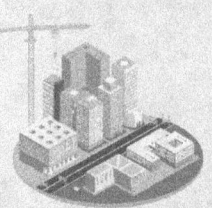

01

02

PAYMENTS AND DISCOUNTS

In this case, builders take money and return the same money to you in instalments as interest. If you ask them for a discount for the projected construction, the builders will take money from you and handover a proportionate discount

03

MONEY IS SECURELY PLACED

This can be beneficial – the money is securely placed away for a long period of time and one gets a steady return over several years

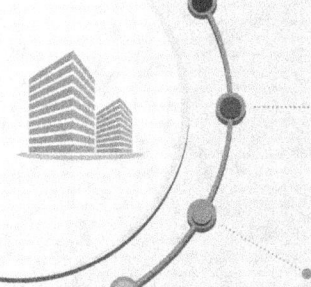

04

HIGH MAINTENANCE COSTS

The maintenance cost from your pocket can be very high – almost Rs. 20 per sq. ft. In case the builders take on the maintenance of the premises, the owner and tenant should get an agreement signed

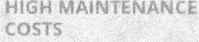

05

OWNERSHIP OF SMALL UNITS

The location of the commercial property is a big factor while selecting where to invest. If it is far from the industrial heart and hub of the area, then it may be difficult to charge a higher rent

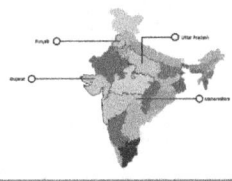

A very favourable rent

The yields per annum!
A very favourable rent can
offer up to 8%. An average
lease runs from 4-5 years.

Industrial hubs in India

Uttar Pradesh, Gujarat, Punjab
and Maharashtra have become
industrial hubs. Currently, Tier I
cities' industrial property is
reaching a point of saturation.

Get Expert Help!

Institutions often turn to industrial
real estate professionals who have
in-depth knowledge and expertise
across various fields like warehouse,
manufacturing and distribution.
Guidance during leasing, buying,
developing, renovating, and also
selling is available from them.

Security is guaranteed

Security is guaranteed since sometimes long term leases and can run up
to 10 years, with fixed yearly increments in price. Industrial leases are
inclusive of maintenance and repair
and also insurance which the owner
has to pay in usual cases.

Buy, Lease or do Both?

Some savvy investors both own
and lease industrial properties in
different locations for stability. The
flexible choices of occupying,
expanding and contracting helps
generate more income.

IMPACT OF GROWING ECONOMY

The Real Estate Sector (Residential, Commercial, Retail and Industrial) has felt the impact of the growing economy directly

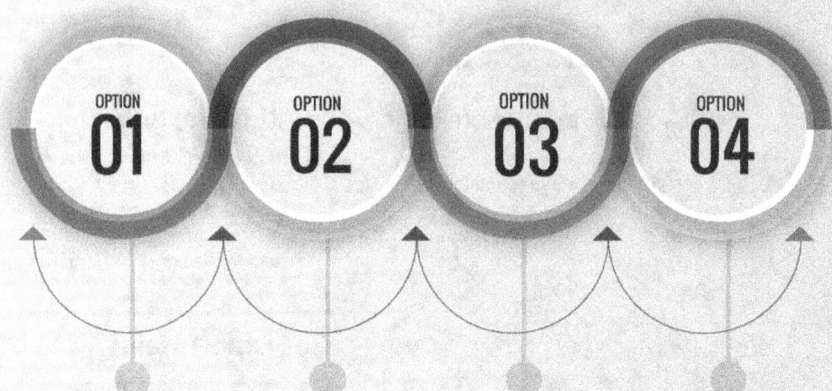

OPTION 01	OPTION 02	OPTION 03	OPTION 04

GDP FROM CONSTRUCTION IN INDIA

Recent figures show that the GDP from Construction in India increased to 2285.27 IND Billion in the first quarter of 2016 from 2213.23 IND Billion in the fourth quarter of 2015. GDP of Construction in India averaged 1975.65 IND Billion from 2011 until 2016. It reached an all time high of 2377.80 IND Billion in the second quarter of 2015

INFRASTRUCTURE OUTPUT

Infrastructure output in the country went up 2.8 percent year-on-year in May of 2016, following an 8.5 percent surge in April while Housing Index averaged 214.69 Index Points from 2011 until 2015, reaching an all time high of 240 Index Points in the fourth quarter of 2014

MOST PREFERRED DESTINATIONS IN ASIA PACIFIC

With the new policies being taken up by the Government of India, including FDI, the Indian real estate market has become one of the most preferred destinations in the Asia Pacific. Overseas funds now account for more than 50 per cent of all investment activity in India in 2014

OFFICE SPACE ABSORPTION

India's office space absorption stood at 35 million square feet during the year2015. This is the second highest figure in the country's history after 2011. This is believed to be driven by corporate implementing their growth plans

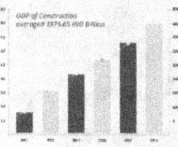

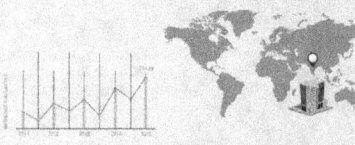

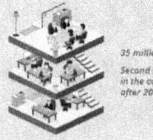

35 million square feet
Second Highest figure in the country's history after 2011

CHAPTER 3

REAL ESTATE INDUSTRY IN THE NEXT DECADE

As per a number of experts from the real estate sector and investment gurus, the real estate sector carries a lot of potential and is sure to deliver astounding results in future. If the current scenario is taken into consideration, there is a major possibility that the assumptions of these experts are indeed true.

There are actually many different things currently happening in India that can benefit the real estate sector in many different ways. Right from the growing economy of the country, 'House for All by 2022' mission of the government, increasing consumerism, digital trends, increasing NRI population, to the multiple initiatives taken by the government, there are several things that favor this sector.

 **However, the expected boom in the sector is easier said than done. As an investor, it is very important to understand how these factors will actually affect the dynamics of the real estate sector in the country and the same is discussed throughout this chapter.**

INDIA'S GROWING ECONOMY AND ITS IMPACT ON THE REAL ESTATE SECTOR (RESIDENTIAL, COMMERCIAL, RETAIL AND INDUSTRIAL)

The current scenario of India's economy, if it can be described in two words, is 'pretty solid'. If we take a peek at the numbers, it will be easier to find out that there is growth in almost every sector. The Gross Domestic Product (GDP) in India increased by 2.10 percent in the first quarter of the year 2016 over the previous quarter.

After a recent survey, the well-known American agency S&P Global Ratings found out that India is well-positioned and praised the Government's "long game" in handling of the economy in order to up the country's growth potential while giving attention to immediate issues as well. The agency made a forecast of 8% growth for the current financial year as well as the next one.

Naturally, the impact of the GDP growth has been elsewhere, in other sectors too.

 Coming directly to the point, the Real Estate Sector (Residential, Commercial, Retail and Industrial) has felt the impact of the growing economy directly.

Recent figures show that the GDP from Construction in India increased to 2285.27 IND Billion in the first quarter of 2016 from 2213.23 IND Billion in the fourth quarter of 2015.

GDP of Construction in India averaged 1975.65 IND Billion from 2011 until 2016. It reached an all-time high of 2377.80 IND Billion in the second quarter of 2015.

Infrastructure output in the country went up 2.8 percent year-on-year in May of 2016, following an 8.5 percent surge in April while Housing Index averaged 214.69 Index Points from 2011 until 2015, reaching an all-time high of 240 Index Points in the fourth quarter of 2014. It may also be noted that the housing sector alone contributes 5-6 per cent to the country's Gross Domestic Product.

With the new policies being taken up by the Government of India, including FDI, the Indian real estate market has become one of the most preferred destinations in the Asia Pacific. Overseas funds accounted for more than 50 per cent of all investment activity in India in 2014.

The growth of the real estate sector is well-complemented by the growth of the corporate environment which naturally demands for office spaces as well as accommodations for urban and semi-urban people. Sectors such as IT and ITeS, retail, consulting and e-commerce have registered a tremendous high demand for office space in recent times.

 **India's office space absorption stood at 35 million square feet during the year 2015. This is the second highest figure in the country's history after 2011. This is believed to be driven by corporations implementing their growth plans.**

With the corporate sector booming, the impact has been various and complementary to each other. With increase in business, there has been an increase in employment. That requires more office space. Side by side, buying power has also increased. Employees need to stay somewhere near their place of work, therefore, residential needs have also increased. With buying power increasing, there has been an increase of retail organizations as well.

HOUSE FOR ALL BY 2022:
A MISSION OR JUST A MANIFESTO

In the last segment, we discussed about the growth of Indian economy and its impact on the real estate sector. Now, we will take a look at a particular scheme connected to real estate, taken up by the Union Government and have a fact check on the pros and cons.

OVERVIEW OF THE HOUSE FOR ALL SCHEME

Recently, in a meeting of the Union Cabinet chaired by the Prime Minister, Shri Narendra Modi, the Cabinet gave approval for the launch of "Housing for All by 2022". The scheme is aimed for urban areas and has the following components/options to be taken up by the States/Union Territories and cities:-

a) Slum rehabilitation of Slum Dwellers with participation of private developers using land as a resource;

b) Promotion of affordable housing for weaker sections through credit-linked subsidy;

c) Affordable housing in partnership with Public & Private sectors

d) Subsidy for beneficiary-led individual house construction or enhancement.

- It was decided that a Central grant of Rs. One lakh per house, on an average, will be available under the slum rehabilitation program.

- The respective State Governments will take the decision in deploying this slum rehabilitation grant to any slum rehabilitation project taken up for development using land as a resource for providing houses to slum dwellers.

- Interest subsidy of 6.5 percent on housing loans availed up to a tenure of 15 years is being provided to EWS/LIG categories, under the Credit-Linked Interest Subsidy component, wherein the subsidy pay-out on NPV basis is about Rs. 2.3 lakh per house for both the categories.

- Central assistance at the rate of Rs. 1.5 lakh per house for EWS category is being provided under the Affordable Housing in Partnership and Beneficiary-led individual house construction or enhancement.

- State Government or their parastatals like Housing Boards can take up the project of affordable housing to avail the Central Government grant.

- The scheme is being implemented as a Centrally-Sponsored Scheme except the credit-linked subsidy component, which is implemented as a Central Sector Scheme.

- The Mission also prescribed certain mandatory reforms for easing up the urban land market for housing, to make adequate urban land available for affordable housing.

- Houses constructed under the mission are allotted in the name of the female head of the households or in the joint name of the male head of the household and his wife.

Now let us take a look at the periphery of the scheme.

The scheme covers the entire urban area consisting of 4041 statutory towns with initial focus on 500 Tier I cities. It was decided that the scheme will be implemented in three phases as follows, viz. Phase-I (April 2015 – March 2017) to cover 100 cities to be selected from States/UTs as per their willingness; Phase – II (April 2017 – March 2019) to cover additional 200 cities and Phase-III (April 2019 – March 2022) to cover all other remaining cities.

The Government will have to spend nearly Rs. 81,975 crore over the construction of these one crore houses in the first three years of the Pradhan Mantri Awaas Yojana-Gramin. The Government is providing financial assistance of Rs. 1.20 lakh to those living in plain areas and Rs. 1.30 lakh to those in "hilly and difficult" areas.

THE SCENARIO AFTER ONE YEAR

Newspaper reports say that a year after the Prime Minister launched the Pradhan Mantri Awaas Yojana (PMAY) with the stated purpose of constructing two crore houses for the urban poor by 2022 — at the rate of 30 lakh houses per year, merely 1,623 houses have been constructed so far.

It was reported that the central funding of Rs. 1 to 1.5 lakh per unit is grossly inadequate for constructing houses in metros such as Mumbai and Delhi and even in many smaller towns.

Coming to the point, it is absolutely clear that red-tape and reluctance of different sectors of the Governmental procedures are denying poor people of their basic rights, however noble the initial scheme is. This is the time, when the Government should directly involve private players in implementation of such schemes, which may be the only way to increase the pace of work.

GROWING NRI POPULATION AND ITS IMPACT ON THE REAL ESTATE SECTOR

It is taken that presently, an estimated 30 million Non-Resident Indians, spread in 160 countries are looking at India for opportunities in real estate investment.

India has been quite consistent in being in the top slot in terms of the quantum of expatriate remittance for years now. The figures in 2010-11 mark India at $55.6 billion, while it was $69 billion in 2015. It has been noticed that a substantial portion of these remittances are forwarded towards investment in real estate across India. A major reason for this is the norms for the NRIs to invest in their motherland have been eased in hugely. The government in recent times has also approved the proposal allowing investments made by NRIs to be treated as domestic investments at par with resident investments.

According to the new norms,

> NRIs who hold land parcels or have inherited property in cities can easily take up ventures in real estate development with leading developers and convert their land into productive as well as income-generating assets.

As a result, luxury apartment projects are being taken up along with ultra-luxury villa projects for non-resident Indians who are accustomed to the luxuries of life abroad.

Thus, an NRI investor can look forward to a return of 20-25% on his investment while investing in such projects. For those NRIs who are looking to invest in leased commercial property, the availability of commercial property investment options is limited, particularly in smaller units.

Let us take a look at the Investment Norms which have been eased for the NRI population.

- The Reserve Bank of India has considerably eased investment norms by NRIs/PIOs who want to invest in real estate. They can buy, sell, gift and inherit immovable property. However, the prohibited categories include agricultural land, plantation property and farmhouses. In the event of sale of immovable property, the authorised dealer may allow repatriation of sale proceeds upto two residential units.
- An NRI/PIO may remit an amount, not exceeding $1 million per financial year out of the balances held in NRO accounts. However, the repatriation is subject to production of documentary evidence in support of acquisition, inheritance or legacy of assets and payment of applicable taxes in India.
- Residents can now remit home loan EMI for NRIs.
- On the taxation front, wealth-tax has been abolished. On the capital gains received while selling immovable property, the cost inflation index will enable NRIs to minimize tax liability. For instance, if an NRI sells a plot of land bought at ₹1 million in 1978 at ₹4 million in 2012-13, resulting in a capital gain of ₹3 million liable for tax, the indexed cost price would be ₹8.5 million, leading to complete exemption from tax.

It may be noted that the depreciation of Indian rupee may largely benefit NRI buyers who are already in the process of finalizing an existing transaction, where their foreign exchange has still not been converted into Indian rupees to pay for their purchase.

There is no denying the fact that Non-Resident Indians are amongst the top five investor communities in India. The slump of the Indian rupee will instigate a cycle that will see a subtle, if not immediate, growth in the real estate sector in the coming days, provided the US dollar continues to remain strong against the Indian rupee.

GROWING CONSUMERISM IN INDIA AND ITS IMPACT ON THE REAL ESTATE SECTOR

India is one of the biggest and fastest growing economies in the world. India is also one of the biggest markets in the world as far as consumer products are concerned. Consumerism basically means the growth of wants and needs of an individual for any kind of goods, products, and services. The consumer's paradigm of life is going higher and therefore there is an obvious escalation of needs. Consumerism in India, is at a new high, and the Indian consumers, due to their exposure to the international market, make every effort to get the best of the goods. The tastes and preferences of Indian consumers are definitely changing, may it be FMCG products or even real estate in a direct or indirect manner.

Positive economic growth has also led to rise in the throwaway income among young professionals and this has, consequently, led to growing interest and objective in real estate sector. Rising consumerism too has proved its positive impact upon retailing and other entertainment avenues, providing the growth of construction of the same.

 **Consumerism in India is largely accountable for the growth of the country's economy in various sectors. One such sector which registered explosive growth is real estate.**

India's real estate market is expected to shoot up to USD 180 billion by 2020 from USD 93.8 billion in 2014. With the emergence of nuclear families, rapid urbanization and rising household, family income remains the key driver for growth in all spheres of real estate sector, including residential, commercial and buildings for retail sector.

Real estate is currently the 4th largest sector in India in terms of Foreign Direct Investment inflows. The total FDI in the construction development sector in the country during April 2000–May 2015 stood at around USD 24 billion.

The Government of India has been encouraging real estate sector. In the year 2015, the Central Government approved 100 Smart City Projects in India. The Union Government has also raised FDI limits for townships and settlements development projects to one hundred per cent. Real estate projects within the Special Economic Zones (SEZ) have also been permitted with 100 per cent FDI.

With the Indian yuppie population on the rise, tech cities being set up, the need for accommodation, retail malls, entertainment centres are inter-connected if not bare necessities. And, all these are the factors for the reality boom. Interestingly, never has anybody ever seen a less conversant purchase than that of a home buyer. It is a dream of many for home ownership and it is driven by passion. This is what bids up the value of properties, thus setting new home records with each buy.

 Prices of houses simply don't go down. The phrase 'Safe as houses' isn't just a myth. It is a fact and a sound one. This is a proposition that always pays back.

Though there has been a recession for four years, out of every 18, as statistics show, the macroeconomic trend goes up to infinity.

Let's take a different view altogether. The most profit-making product isn't the iPhone 7. It's real estate. This is the ultimate in the sphere of consumerism. The property prices bubble never bursts.

DIGITAL TRENDS IMPACTING THE REAL ESTATE SECTOR

The current scenario of marketing is hugely influenced by Internet-based services as well as social media. With more than half of the urban Indian population, presumably consumers, connected to the Internet through their smart phones, reaching out and creating an impact is a click away, for any product. The real estate sector is not out of bounds for such marketing strategies and many of the companies are now bearing the fruits of success.

> Real estate players including Godrej Properties, Tata Housing and Adani have joined the bandwagon of digital media marketing in a process to strengthen sales. From hiring social media marketing firms to setting up YouTube channel for the brand which showcases walkthroughs of upcoming projects, there are unlimited ways to create impact upon the consumers.

Not only are the real estate developers finding digital media very cost-efficient but also much more effective in enhancing conversion rates.

Statistics show that Tata Housing received more than 10 bookings within hours after going live on the Internet while Godrej Properties has 20% of its sales through online marketing.

 **The Internet is powering consumer behavior as 7 out of 10 buyers now know about the exact brand or the model they wish to buy, through the researches made by them online. This came up in a study by Google India.**

Many developers found success recently in the three-day 'Great Online Shopping Festival' where an association between Google and Tata Housing had prospective buyers being offered houses and encouraged them to book a flat or apartment by the company. Moreover, Tata Value Homes (TVHL), recently received more than 200 applications online hours after the event, National Home Buying Day.

The number of online enquiries for Godrej Properties, regarding its projects has more than doubled over the recent times.

The developers can now organize contests on Google+ and LinkedIn and get connected with customers from different strata. There is also the integrated IP-based calling, connected to their call centers. Here people are trained to work upon campaign-related enquiries. Developers are now taking help of professional digital media marketing firms in order to enhance their web presence.

 **What also has been attracting real estate developers to the platform is that it is cost-efficient, compared to advertorials in prints, hoardings or audio-visual advertisements on television.**

Digital media tends to cost one-tenth of the conventional print and outdoor platforms. Yet, it brings in at least 40-45 per cent conversions and the numbers are only growing.

Let's discuss five basic strategies

STRATEGY 1 – MARKETING SHOULD BE CREATIVE

The WOW factor is an important point and the digital marketing team you have entrusted your campaign to, must make you different from the others. Here it is not the frequency of updates that matter but the quality.

STRATEGY 2 – A MONTHLY MARKETING PLAN IS A MUST

Plan the content and promotion process of the content on a monthly basis, if not on a weekly basis. Check the feedback and suggestions and see how worthy or logical they are in future aspects.

STRATEGY 3 – A LEAD READY REAL ESTATE WEBSITE IS THE NEED OF THE HOUR

Get rid of templates. Go dynamic. Install Calls-To-Action for your customers. Give stress to blogging.

STRATEGY 4 – GIVE EMPHASIS ON SEO

Search Engine Optimization is an important factor to bring you up in the front and stay visible.

STRATEGY 5 – GIVE PREFERENCE TO EMAIL MARKETING

Once a strong email list is ready, be sure to have it nurtured. Email marketing is always effective, provided done in a proper manner. Make sure your emails are optimized for mobile phones too.

GOVERNMENT INITIATIVES IN THE REAL ESTATE SECTOR

The Union Budget 2016 had much to cheer about for the reality sector. The Union Finance Minister Arun Jaitley removed the last significant tax hurdle which was in the way of Real Estate Investment Trusts (REITs), gave incentives to first-time home buyers and even tried to make affordable housing much more viable.

> **The 2016 Budget left out REITs—listed entities that primarily invest in leased office and retail assets, thus allowing the developers to raise funds by selling completed properties to investors and in the process, listing them as a trust—from the purview of dividend distribution tax (DDT).**

In the last two budgets, the Central Government has worked on easing the path for REIT listing in India. It has done so by providing pass-through status for rental income and has rationalized capital gains for the sponsors in different conditions. The biggest beneficiaries of REITs are companies which have large rent generating, commercial office portfolios.

In order to address housing needs of the poor, housing activity under the Pradhan Mantri Awaas Yojna, has been implemented by this government and the Finance Minister has proposed to give 100%

deduction for profits to undertakings from housing projects for flats up to a certain area in four metro cities and certain areas in other cities, in the current Budget. The projects have to be approved between June 2016 to March 2019 and completed within three years of the approval.

Minimum Alternate Tax or MAT will be applied to these undertakings. Exemption of service tax on construction of affordable houses up to a certain area has also been proposed under a scheme of the Central or State Government. This includes public-private partnership schemes.

"For the first-time home buyers, I propose to give deduction for additional interest of Rs. 50,000 per annum for loans up to Rs. 35 lakh sanctioned during the next financial year, provided the value of the house does not exceed Rs. 50 lakh," the Union Finance Minister said in his Budget speech.

Major boost for Real Estate sector during the last two years –

SMART CITY:
The Proposal: With a vision to bring a new horizon of urban growth, the Government has proposed to build 100 smart cities in India. A list of 98 cities has been declared out of which 33 cities have already been chosen over two rounds. The Government has so far allocated around Rs. 48,000 crores as seed funding.

HOUSING FOR ALL BY 2022
The present Government has proposed to build houses for all the people belonging to the Economically Weaker Section (EWS) & Lower Income Group (LIG) who do not have houses. The initiative will provide interest subsidies and financial aid and has the vision to build around 110 million individual units by 2022.

REITS: ENABLING RETAIL INVESTMENT IN THE INDIAN COMMERCIAL SECTOR
Through Real Estate Investment Trust, small investors are able to invest in income-generating commercial real estate units. The Government

has been taking policy-based initiatives to expedite the process for implementing REITs in the Indian market.

REAL ESTATE REGULATORY ACT

With the objective of bringing transparency in the overall Indian real estate industry, the present Government has brought a proposal for a string of regulations in the form of a new law, the Real Estate Regulation Act. The Act will make it mandatory for the developer to share all the relevant information regarding projects with the Real Estate Regulatory Act (RERA).

CHAPTER 4

UPCOMING CHALLENGES ONE SHOULD KNOW ABOUT

While there are many different factors that appear to be in favor of the real estate sector in India, there are many others that can prove to be unfavorable. Some of these factors are the mismatch of supply and demand, black money and its flow in the country, and the increasing burden of taxes on the middle class.

Although the appreciation has somewhat stabilized, the rental yield is still very low and this is highly discouraging for the investors who are looking to buy a property to let it out on rent. While government is expected to play a major role in tackling these negative factors and people have high hopes from the current government, there is still a very long way to go before declaring this sector a completely safe form of investment that can provide significant returns in future.

> Apart from the things that can benefit the sector, it is also important to know about the factors that can negatively impact it to make sure that every investor only makes a decision after knowing the positives as well as the negatives.

THE DEMAND SUPPLY MISMATCH (HIGH INVENTORY)

Recently, examples of firms suffering from excess inventory and issues related to supply chain management have been discussed by many practitioners and academicians.

Although excess inventory is probable to have a negative effect on the performance of a firm, there is a modest systematic analysis of the degree of performance effects due to excess inventory and therefore the determinants of the effects of performance. Given the fundamental role of inventory management, this is quite surprising in research and practice of operations management. Its evidence is based on analysis made from 276 excess inventory announcements which were found out from some publicly traded firms during the period 1990–2002. These announcements have been acknowledged by firms that are suffering from excess of inventories.

Examples vary from channel inventory build-up, curtailment of production, temporary shutdowns, promotions and markdown as well as writing off inventories to deal with the excess.

 **Some of the products with less volume of demand often experience momentous demand changeability. This leads to an increase in inventory. Other products may act in opposite direction, experiencing steady demand with very little disparity.**

This question has surpassed industry as well as geographic location. However, the answer remains indefinable for most organisations. In an effort to provide an answer and to address the common deal between inventory and customer service levels, a framework is proposed which will align supply chain operations with the corresponding demand.

The framework has some definite principles:
1) Both the quantity and changeability of demand must be taken into account. This is called volume-variability demand profiling.
2) Product manufacturing and distribution should be at par with this profile through strategies leading to a mix of build-to-stock, build-to-order and make-to-order.

Getting more success in the marketplace these days is dependent on solving the question that has plagued almost every Monday morning meeting for countless ages—How can one optimize inventory while maintaining high levels of service?

A scholar and master in this field opines that there is a sustainable competitive advantage for whoever figures that out first.

A case study can demonstrate a company's response. Instead of blindly putting into practice a make-to-stock operational strategy for all products across the board, firms can utilize a best-fit, multi-tier manufacturing and distribution method. However, implementation of the right operational policy depends heavily on understanding the demand for a product and not just its volume but also its changeability.

 **There are companies that understand the demand of their products and thus, adapt both the manufacturing and distribution policies in accordance to achieve a win-win situation of better service to customers and lower inventory positions.**

One can definitely argue that these principles may not work in all industries or in generalised forms. However, it may surely be taken to some extent where all companies can apply the basic concepts of volume and variability profiling regardless to which sector of industries they belong to. For example, even firms in the most complex industrial sectors, for example, say aerospace—can put into action these concepts to their basic SKUs and common components. All companies can get advantage from using volume-variability demand profiling at the very least, to identify the manufacturing and distributional approach that can deal with their supply-demand mismatch in the best manner.

CURBING BLACK MONEY FLOW AND ITS IMPACT

It is a fact that there is no reliable information about the money of Indians in undisclosed bank accounts which is out of reach of the jurisdiction of our country. There have been estimates made of various degrees but all based on assumptions or presumptions. A proposal has already been approved by the Government of India for conducting a study to estimate the quantum of black money that exists both inside and outside the country.

The Government of India has devised a five-pronged policy to deal with the hazard of black money which is as below:

  (i)   Joining the global crusade against black money,
  (ii) Creating an appropriate legislative framework,
  (iii) Setting up institutions for dealing with Illicit Funds,
  (iv) Developing systems for implementation (new manpower policy); and
  (v)   Imparting skills to manpower for effective action (regular training for skill development).

We will discuss the steps taken by the GOI and its impacts one by one.

1. JOINING THE GLOBAL CRUSADE AGAINST BLACK MONEY:

There are no geo-political boundaries for black money. It is a global problem. Global efforts are being made against curbing black money and India is playing a proactive part in pointing out paucities in the assessment of various countries through the Peer Review Group of the Global Forum.

 **India became a member of the Task Force on Financial Integrity and Economic Development so that it can be more transparent and accountable regarding the financial system.**

India has joined different forums like the Financial Action Task Force (FATF), the Asia Pacific Group (APG) against Money laundering, the Eurasian Group (EAG), the Egmont Group which is an international network fostering improved communication and interaction among Financial Intelligence Units (FIU) and has been an active member of G-20 where it has played a key role in identifying issues and also drafting communiqués.

2. CREATING AN APPROPRIATE LEGISLATIVE FRAMEWORK:

The Government of India is on a path to strengthen the legislative framework so that the generation of black money in the country can be controlled along with flight of illicit fund to tax-havens.

Keeping with the pace, our country has so far concluded negotiations of 22 new Tax Information Exchange Agreements with various tax-havens. Many of these agreements have also been approved by the Union Cabinet.

Processes of negotiation have been initiated by our country with 75 other countries so as to broaden the scope of the Article concerning Exchange of Information to purposely allow exchange of banking information.

A protocol amending India's tax treaty with Switzerland was signed in 2010 and it has been approved of late by the Swiss Parliament. Soon, the DTAA will become operational. It will enter into force when Switzerland completes its internal process.

3. SETTING UP INSTITUTIONS FOR DEALING WITH ILLICIT FUNDS:

An Exchange of Information (EoI) Cell is being set up by the Government of India so that effective exchange of information may be made possible in order to limit tax evasion. The cell is to be placed under Foreign Tax Division of CBDT.

The creation of the Directorate of Income Tax (Criminal Investigation), in the Central Board of Direct Taxes has also been approved by the Government. The DCI will take up criminal matters which may have financial implications punishable as an offence under any direct tax law.

 Income tax Overseas Units have been set up by the Government in two Indian Missions abroad. Eight more such units are being setup in foreign countries.

4. DEVELOPING SYSTEMS FOR IMPLEMENTATION:

The strength of Foreign Tax Division has been doubled to deal with proper exchange of information.

The Directorate of International Taxation as well as Transfer Pricing in the Income Tax Department have been strengthened as major part of the surge of black money outside of India takes place through mispricing of foreign transactions.

5. IMPARTING SKILLS TO THE MANPOWER FOR EFFECTIVE ACTION:

As a part of capacity building and skill development, many senior officers have been sent abroad for specialized training in the field of International Taxation and Transfer Pricing.

Since skill upgradation in such matters is a time-taking process, a posting policy has been approved by the Government of India.

INCREASING TAX BURDEN ON THE MIDDLE CLASS

The Indian Middle class has been a loser in most of the tax reforms by the Government. Besides direct taxes, the burden of indirect taxes has troubled the household and their petty savings. The last Union Budget had shattered the expectations for tax relief.

Roundabout 3.5 crore people in India pay income tax and surprisingly, the number is less than 3% of the total population of the country. Out of the 3.5 crore people, more than 50% pay tax in the range of Rs. 50-1,000 as income tax , the revenue earned is negligible. This leaves just 1.5 to 1.75 crore of tax payers.

Now, these are educated and salaried class of people who pay their taxes and contribute their hard-earned money for the progress of the country. And they have no option as whatever their earning is, it is tax deducted at source.

Now, let's come to numbers.

 **While corporate taxes have been taken to grow by 8.4% in the FY 2016-17 only, it is expected that personal income tax collections will grow by 17 per cent in the FY 2016-17.**

Even after 68 years of Independence, there have been no substantial steps taken to augment the tax net/base. Government data says that 0.9

per cent agriculturists pay income tax. Just 1 per cent of the population of India accounts for 12.6 per cent of gross national income, says the Economic Survey 2016. While just 1% or roundabout 1.27 crore people are responsible for the Government's revenue; only 42,800 people in India actually declare income of over Rs. 1 crore.

Let's have a look at the latest budget, and how it made an impact on the Middle class.

The indirect taxes have put an additional burden of Rs. 20,600 crore on the middle class consumers in the coming financial year.

Prices of tobacco products have gone up due to increase in excise duties on tobacco products from 10 to 15 per cent. Power tariff has gone up by Rs. 400 per tonne as the Government increased the 'Clean Environmental Cess' on coal, lignite and peat.

The Finance Minister has introduced a few new cesses such as Krishi Kalyan Cess of 0.5% on all taxable services. This has made eating out expensive as the service tax is now being levied at 15%.

 **Consumers are now paying more telephone bills, more money for air tickets, for insurance premium and while buying property. It is a pity for the middle class that the introduction of new cesses, in addition to those which are existing has only made the consumables dearer.**

The Finance Minister also made changes in customs and excise duty rates on certain inputs. Jewellery and branded garments are now subjected to Central Excise Duty of 1 per cent and 2 per cent respectively.

The last union budget also made provisions for increase in service tax, which essentially made everything more expensive for the common man. For the first time, Provident Fund has been made taxable thus adding to the misery of the service class.

Adding more misery to the middle class, recently, the government cut the interest rates on offer on the PPF or the public provident fund and other small savings schemes run by the post office.

LOW RENTAL YIELD: A DETERRENT FOR INVESTORS (ESPECIALLY AS APPRECIATION HAS STABILIZED)

Recent market surveys in major Indian cities depict that prices of residential property have risen strongly and sharply. However, if we take a look at the graphic comparisons, regarding rental properties, the gross rental yield - i.e., the percentage return on the purchase of property, is abysmally low in major cities.

South Mumbai depicts very low rental yields, with property investors getting return of around 2.40%-3.5% gross.

In New Delhi, the prices of properties per sq. m. are, of course, comparatively lower, despite the incessant price-rises. Gross rental yield as far as New Delhi is concerned, is poor and lies between 2.88% to 3.20%.

In Bangalore, the rental yields are higher, ranging from 3.33% to 4.04%, but low compared to 2007, when it was between 7.16% and 9.92%.

THE GENERAL SCENARIO

{ **The investment return on residential properties by means of rentals in tier 1 cities in our country is among the lowest in the world. As we have seen above, the rental yields in Delhi are the lowest while Mumbai fares better.**

According to a report by global real estate consultancy Jones Lang LaSalle (JLL), the rent return in the Indian market is little in spite of the fact that owning a real estate asset in India is unsafe, as a World Bank study says. However, local as well as international investors have great attraction towards Indian real estate sector for their investments.

Economists and financial consultants are of the opinion that in emerging economies, investors put funds into the real estate sector for greater return from capital appreciation. As a result, the universal norm of high risk-high return is not applicable to investments made in residential real estate sector in India and other developing nations.

WHAT THE RENTAL YIELDS POINT OUT

It is interesting to know that the annual rate of return through acquired rental income from any residential property at the current price which is actually the rental yield, in developed countries is much higher than that is in countries having emerging economies. Also, if rental yields are put in comparison with the opportunity cost of funds, which may be taken as an equal to the interest that the identical money can get if it is invested as a fixed deposit with any bank, in reality, the rental yields always fetch a far superior return.

However, in India, the rental yield is close to 30-40% of the fixed deposit rates. In most of the emerging markets, especially in South East Asia, in places like Jakarta and Manila, rental yields are superior than the fixed deposits rate.

On the contrary, owning a house in places like Manila or Jakarta has a greater risk factor than that in India.

Indian gross rental yields are extremely low. From this, one can get the idea that Indian residential property maybe overvalued. Though low rental yields do not at all times point to over-valuation, especially at the times when interest rates are low, they are only acceptable if brisk economic growth is expected.

This also happens if there are adequate restrictions on new building construction to avert the market being swarmed with new properties during price rise.

It is quite clear that a buyer or an investor should keep eyes and ears open and follow up researches before taking a leap. It is a fact however, that in India, local policies influence the rental yield and a generalized view is devoid of the whole picture. What is necessary is a thorough research on the geographical juncture where the investment may be made and at most times, one can hit a jackpot.

LAND ACQUISITION: A HERCULEAN TASK FOR THE REAL ESTATE DEVELOPERS

Land acquisition for real estate development, may it either be for industrial cause or housing, is a very serious issue where there is no question of any short-cuts. If something regarding a land deal for any project seems to be out of place, then one can be rest assured that there is an issue with the land, over any other factors.

> With newer legislations being made and the Government showing interest in projects like Smart Cities, the purpose of buying land for development is expected to be getting a clean and secure title and then being able to build up on the plot without facing any complications in the future at the development stage, and doing it in a stipulated timeframe.

A NIGHTMARE FOR THE DEVELOPERS

In the entire muddle of problems which are related to land for real estate, it is the developers who face the greatest challenge in obtaining an undisputed, bankable title to an adjacent land parcel of having the necessary dimensions and qualities to develop a project. The other issue they face is the loss of cost control during the process of acquisition. It has often been seen that the cost of acquisition after completion of the entire process of acquiring is so high that the development becomes an expensive affair.

There have been many instances in which the developers have been able to solve the problems involved in the acquisition and development of land through pooling of respective land, wherein, a number of land owners have been made to agree to pool their holdings of land and thus develop their total land altogether.

Amanora and Magarpatta, in Pune have been developed into townships in such manner, giving impetus to Pune's IT industry.

THE ROLE OF THE GOVERNMENT

It is quite difficult to get a 100% clean land parcel of any noteworthy size according to the present laws. The present law on real estate does not have provisions to discourage a claimant from moving to the courts at any period and at any occasion. The only safe way to procure land with a 100% secure title in the country was through the Government. However, with farmers going to court at Noida West and Greater Noida, in Singur in West Bengal, even that course is now a questionable one. In order to make land acquiring in India easier, the Government needs to legislate proactive laws for the procedure of acquisition, side by side the processes of resettlement and rehabilitation of those whose lands are being acquired.

The two most significant needs at this time are firstly to do away with the Urban Land Ceiling Act across the country and to formulate and legislate laws encouraging participation of the owner in development of land.

The Government should take the responsibility to provide land for development, besides on rehabilitation and resettlement. Cases like Singur, Greater Noida and Noida West must be avoided at all costs, as they ward off global confidence of investing in India.

PART 2

STARTING YOUR REAL ESTATE INVESTMENT

CHAPTER 1

CHOOSING THE RIGHT TYPE OF
REAL ESTATE INVESTMENT

Investing in the real estate sector has become highly popular in the last few decades in India due to the improving economic condition of the country. However, investing in the real estate sector is a lot more than just simply searching for a good location and buying a property.

> While the sector is indeed very promising, especially in India, buying a real estate property is much more complicated as compared to investing in stocks or bonds. This is mainly due to the fact that this sector is still largely unorganized, the investors have minimum amount of knowledge about real estate and there is huge amount of money involved in the transactions.

It is very important for every investor to first understand their needs from a real estate sector investment to narrow down the available choices. Selecting between residential and commercial properties, diversifying the investments and having clear idea about the future of real estate sector in India are some of the points that can help investors make the right decision. All these important factors will be discussed in detail in this chapter.

IDENTIFY YOUR NEED

Making investment in the real estate sector is perhaps one of the most profitable ventures anywhere in the world. In India, investment in land, apartment, farm or even commercial real estate has been in practice since many years. Though, the rent output is much lesser if Indian metro cities are compared with any other city in the world, the trend of investing in real estate continues to be the primary form of investment in our country.

WHAT SHOULD BE THE RIGHT CHOICE?

There are plenty of investment opportunities in the market, starting from a high risk share market and mutual funds to low risk government schemes, the only difference being the return rate. While share markets can offer high return in little time, Government schemes and bonds provide low interest rate in greater time frame, but the risk factor is negligible. But again, if real estate is taken into account, we should first get an idea about what the market is like by reading a small story that appeared in a newspaper a few months back:

> The iconic Lincoln House in Mumbai was, of late, bought by an industrialist for Rs. 750 crore. The Lincoln House is a 50,000 sq. ft property and had been leased to the US Government by the Maharaja of Wankaner, for Rs. 18 lakh in 1957. Since then, in the past 58 years, the value of this property has grown 4,000-times, at an annual growth rate of 15.45%.

Now, this is not the only case in India but a generalized version of what real estate can really fetch. Our parents had much more faith in real estate than in the equity market and they were not wrong.

It is very necessary to find what exactly what should be the right choice for you, depending upon the risk factor you want to associate yourself with. Obviously, there are risk factors in real estate too, depending upon the nature of the property, its surroundings and locality and political interference, if any. Now let us take a stroll towards the risk factor. Buying an under-construction flat is definitely not a real estate investment. By doing so, you are in fact lending money to a developer with a high hope that he may deliver a flat to you in the near future. You might get a good return when you buy an under-construction flat. Return follows risk, and in the Indian context, the risks of buying an under-construction flat are very high, so much so that developers have to endow with a price that gives you good returns. In spite of all these facts, if you pick the right one at the right time, surely the return figures should make you a satisfied man.

IDENTIFY YOUR NEED

You have to identify your need. If you want a second home, which you will hardly want to sell, real estate investment is not the one for you. However, the general trend is buying flats and then when the area is more developed, with amenities such as newly-built flyovers, roads or full-functioning metro lines, selling the property and making a grand profit. It is a question of intuition and research put together to identify the need of the hour and to act accordingly, because one needs to make the best from the few chances he gets.

DIVERSIFICATION IS THE NEED OF THE HOUR

Diversification is another word for success only when your confidence allows you to seek for growth. Growth is necessary for all those who aspire to do something in life. Growth is like oxygen that helps people exist and dream for success and a better life. Without diversification growth is not possible, neither in business, nor in investments.

TYPES OF INVESTMENTS WE GENERALLY GO FOR

Investment in equity is perhaps the most popular form of investment for those who like to take risks in the open market. However, those with a traditional mindset would go for investment in real estate on any given opportunity. With the equity market or the real estate market, the desired growth is achievable. Well, there are risk factors, but that is where the game is; matching intelligence with the market and winning.

HOW DO WE DIVERSIFY?

Let's make an assumption that we have been only investing in the stock market or mutual funds all these days and have been getting pretty good returns. Now, there is an urge to explore newer avenues and get more out of it. Then, where do we go? This is a big question and it has a simple answer. There is always the chance to venture into real estate investments.

> **Properties are assets that can be banked for even when the equity market reaches rock-bottom. Investments in gold and silver, however, are the only other winners, besides real estate.**

WHY IS REAL ESTATE AN OPTION FOR DIVERSIFICATION?

If you consider the trend of rising prices of property over the last five years, the price of the property you have picked out will keep going up along with time, at the best expectations. Residential real estate is an asset class whose prices have been progressively rising in most of the markets. Financial analysts are of an opinion that the residential property market in locations such as the Delhi-NCR, Bengaluru and Mumbai is fully grown for a price correction, where property developers have been able to cling on to their prices even as buyers are waiting for a fall in prices. Given the imbalance in demand-supply, the tendency is likely to persist and your investment, will in all possibility, rise up to an unforeseen height even when other assets are taking a beating.

If we consider the past few years, the data shows that real estate belongs to a rewarding asset class. If we take examples, 2011 has been one of the worst years for equities as Sensex fell almost by 25%. However in the same year, the prices of homes in most Indian cities remained fixed in spite of the overall financial and economic doldrums, both in the international and domestic markets.

> **If we consider the National Housing Bank's residential index, or the Residex, prices of real estate in 9 out of 15 cities rose during the year, except in Ahmedabad, where prices remained the same.**

In comparison, if you had made investment in real estate stocks in the same period, the value of your investment would have dropped by nearly 50% between December 2010 and December 2011.

Real estate prices have outperformed equities, currency as well as bonds by a broad margin. As long as the Indian economy goes on growing and Indians continue to gain the power of purchasing, prices are likely to continue to rise as far as real estate is concerned.

RESIDENTIAL V/S COMMERCIAL

Investing in either residential or commercial real estate is an evident choice for any of the real estate investors. But there are fundamental differences between these asset classes.

At times, one needs to make a choice between either residential or commercial real estate investment in India and some consider that residential real estate does have an edge. In major Indian cities, it is common to have an excess demand for housing units, and it is this demand that drives up the price of real estate. As a result, the real estate investors of the country prefer to invest in residential real estate.

> There is always the assurance that there will be a steady rental income. There is the scope of capital appreciation as well.

BASIC DIFFERENCE IN RESIDENTIAL AND COMMERCIAL REAL ESTATE

Firstly, the price of commercial property is a multiple of the price of residential real estate. Yes, you can buy individual shops or even small offices at prices that can be compared with the likes of residential properties, but the cost of hefty, quality commercial real estate such as shopping malls, office blocks or industrial premises may run into hundreds of crores of rupees.

Secondly, most commercial properties that are not exactly within the city boundaries or even industrial warehouses are properties which the investors find difficult to get accurate valuations of without the help of professional consultation. On the contrary, investment in residential real estate is comparatively an easy job as the prices of houses or flats in a given area can easily be compared.

Thirdly, there are significant differences in the lease of license between the landlord and tenant when comparing cases of commercial and residential properties. The basics are given below:

- **Commercial leases generally last much longer compared to residential leases. While at least a period of five years is normal for commercial properties, periods of 11 months to one year renewable residential leases are generally set.**

- **In case of commercial property, in general, rent can't be less after renewal as compared to what it was before renewal.**

- **The legal agreement between the landlord and tenant is different for commercial and residential lease deeds.**

- **The terms and conditions in the license deed for repairs and maintenance are different in commercial properties than in that of residential properties. The landlords are normally responsible for repair and maintenance in the latter.**

- **Residential real estate also possibly requires more management time compared to that of commercial property. This is because of the unit size being smaller, the lease lengths being shorter and the obligation for maintenance and repairs being present.**

For an investor, there are two most significant initial costs of acquiring the property and the return on investment. A good residential property may be lesser in price but may be unable to fetch higher returns. Whereas, a 700 sq. ft. commercial property at a good location will cost around Rs. 50 lakhs and might provide a return of around Rs. 50 thousand monthly. This goes to show that the proceeds are higher in commercial real estate than in residential properties.

THE ROAD AHEAD FOR RETAIL SPACES

The Indian Retail sector has been at the helm of India's growth story and has gone through many transformations over the last decade. There has been a noticeable shift in this country towards organised retailing. The US global management consulting firm A.T. Kearney recently ranked India as the fourth most attractive nation for retail investment among 30 flourishing markets. From traditional *kirana* stores to rural fairs, from Mama-Papa shops to convenience shops and plush malls, from stores of retail brands' outlets to multinational giant shops, there has been a massive growth in this country. As a result, the demand for commercial properties has increased by leaps and bounds.

> **The Indian economy started to open its doors to foreign brands in 1991 which resulted in a change in retailing. The retail market might possibly reach a whooping Rs. 47 lakh crore by 2016-17, says a 'Yes Bank - Assocham' study. The retail market (including organised and unorganised retail) was at Rs. 23 lakh crore in 2011-12. The study says that organised retail, that comprised just 7% of the overall retail market in 2011-12, may possibly grow at a CAGR of 24% and attain 10.2% share of the total retail sector by 2016-17.**

In terms of space, organised retail in 2013 occupied around 4.7 million sq. ft. This is an increase of around 78% over the total mall space of about 2.5 million sq ft in 2012.

The factors behind this huge surge can be summarized as favourable demographics, more nuclear families, increased urbanisation tendency, growing fondness for branded products, etc.

MARKET DYNAMICS

The Indian Retail sector has seen a massive growth in the organised segment in the last few years. Prominent domestic players have stepped into the arena of retail with long term and determined plans to expand their business in every known format, in every possible city.

The newest trend in organised retail is the virtual format where customers can place orders online and the products are delivered at the door step. This trend has been catching up. Thus, besides retail properties in malls, the need for space for warehousing has also increased manifold.

RETAIL SPACES

India is expected to attract $75-80 million of private equity as investment in the retail real estate sector in 2016, according to latest reports. The Foreign Direct Investment or FDI inflow into retail trading has increased between October 2014 and September 2015 to $70.75 million.

The expectancy over private equity inflows comes along with economic stability in addition to Government's liberalisation of the FDI policy. Consumer sentiments also play a huge part, though. Our country is also witnessing a sharp rise in consumer desire to use foreign brands as brand awareness has increased.

The entry of more and more multinationals including H&M, Wendy's has resulted in a growing need for constructing world-class malls, which have unmatched designs as well as ambience. This should lead to materialization of stronger retail real estate that might manage to acquire private equity (PE) investment in future.

CHAPTER 2

PREPARATION IS THE KEY

While tips from a friend or relative who has recently invested in a real estate property should be taken into consideration, it is important for every real estate investor to do their own preparation before making a decision. This is basically due to the different needs of different investors.

While your friend or relative might have actually made a great decision for themselves, there is a possibility that their strategy might not provide you with the results you are looking for. It is only the preparation that an investor does himself as per his investment needs that can help him make the right decision.

Right from selecting a property, understanding the role of brokers, to managing the finances, every aspect of real estate investment should be thoroughly analyzed before taking any decision. While this was complicated in the past, Internet has opened the door of knowledge for everyone and investors can find useful knowledge in abundance, online. All the important aspects for preparing an investor are explained in this chapter.

THE ROLE OF BROKERS IN THE REALTY SECTOR

As far as the Indian realty sector is concerned, people in general, looked down upon the property brokerage profession. It was thought that property brokerage was an affair for people who could do nothing else. However, such atrocious idea has eventually lost roots and property brokerage firms are, at this juncture respectable businesses, fetching huge profit to the entrepreneurs. With FDI being introduced in the Indian real estate, real estate brokerage is now a lucrative job and a booming one as well.

Brokers play a significant role in real estate sector. Besides being the facilitator of the deal, the broker is also the trust-maker between the buyer and the seller. Surely, small deals like renting an apartment or a shop can be executed without the help of a broker, but when the size and the worth of the land increases, it is then that one can understand the value of a real estate broker. It is the broker who will be helping in paper-work: such as organizing all the papers for registration, title deeds, certificates stating no dues are left to be paid and host of other legalities. The broker will help in providing the information regarding current market prices, and the potential of the property in the future corresponding to the local market. Here, the only sensible thing a buyer or a seller can do is to get the right broker by checking his credentials.

> **The general trend is - when it comes to house-hunting, most have the dilemma of whether they should go or not go through a broker and clinch a deal.**

The important information to share is that, in recent times, bigger players like Tata Housing and RIC have joined hands for setting up a stage for providing training to brokers in the real estate sector.

An agent-only directory website has come into existence to help people find their desired properties. Such elite portals for real estate consultants have their complete profiles on display. Real estate as a category is highly disjoint. Consumers go online to service their necessities. At this juncture, it is necessary for brokers to be ready to upgrade and relate to present technology. If a broker is registered in such elite directories, which are subscription-based, deals will automatically be fruitful.

At this point of time, a broker should convert his business from simply brokerage to a full-fledged consultancy service. Such steps will help in organising a consultant's work, besides providing all the required tools for marketing and branding.

> **If we go by the various data available from the industry, about 15-25% of all real estate deals now come from the online environment. Brokers have played a vital role in the development and growth of the real estate market in India. Training them would further build up their value and make them competent in making decisions.**

It is true that in the past, despite playing significant roles in the buying cycle, brokers never acquired the respect due to them because of the huge break in the expectation of service of the customer. The credit for the development of the real estate industry should be given to brokers as they play a decisive role in the buying cycle of a consumer.

TAKING ADVANTAGE OF
THE ONLINE WORLD

In this world of Internet communication, one thing all the real estate agents should ensure is that they have a proper and active presence online. Online communication is the in-thing while the age-old simple signpost – a handshake is a thing of the past. Well, no need to discard it though, as human contact, tête-à-tête meetings are of supreme importance when big deals are finalized. However, it is a fact that online real estate has grown more than the actual property itself. Potential buyers like to experience their dream home even before they are scheduled for inspection. Buyers should be able to recognize what is great about the property as well as the neighbourhood and should be made to develop an interest in the property before they have even walked through the door.

Here are some marketing tips for online real estate which can assist you to win customers even before they enter the front door of any property.

Pinterest: Making a Pinterest page for your properties individually can do wonders and attract your clientele as you can take as many pictures as you want to show off the property and its amenities. You can even include images of the neighbouring attractions that surround the property. Buying and selling of home is a visual experience and, therefore, Pinterest can be used to the fullest by the real estate agents.

Facebook: Facebook is the in-thing and everybody is a part of it. You can portray your agency, upload pictures of your property and side by side get connected to your clientele in an informal way. You can even use the paid service to boost up your posts and reach out to many others.

Webpage: Web pages are an important medium to portray your properties. It is better if you can build webpage for an individual home or an area where you have multiple listings. By doing so, web pages become an amazing online real estate tool. Again, it is also necessary to promote your website across your other social media profiles such as Twitter and Facebook.

YouTube: Try to narrate a walkthrough of one of your homes for sale and upload the video on YouTube. Videos are an incredible way for buyers to feel like they have truly experienced a feel of the property before they have stepped through the door. Do not forget to publicize your YouTube video through other social media networks.

LinkedIn: LinkedIn is a great network for commercial real estate if you are in that market as business owners and professionals have the propensity to be very active on LinkedIn. This is a formal platform and posts should be very professional and to the point.

Message Boards: Finally, you need to have a message board where customers will be able to post comments, chat about the neighbourhood or enquire directly to you about a property. This is a useful online real estate tool for you to use. Do check back in with people at periodic intervals to see what they are saying about your properties.

Online real estate is here to stay and grow. It is high time to use these online real estate tools and take advantage of these effective marketing options

MANAGING YOUR CASH FLOW AND FINANCES

For any new business, the first few years are very crucial to its success. There are many challenges to overcome and lessons to be learnt in the process.

Some of the major causes of business failure in the first few years are cash flow problems and mismanaged finances. While there are companies who fail to plan properly, there are some who set their sights wrong, too high or low. While some companies don't keep track of costs, there are some who fail to get payment.

You can make the most of your chances of success in business by being conscious of the drawbacks. Then you can manage your company's finances cautiously and keep a vigilant eye on its cash flow.

Practical steps will help you to be in command and develop your business without taking unnecessary risks in financial matters. Here are some useful tips you may consider:

- **Use financial planning and forecasting: It is always useful to build up a financial plan or a structure so that you can keep a track of finances.**

- **Set cash flow targets:** You can control cash flow by preparing and maintaining a cash flow plan which may be updated weekly or in a periodic manner in order to provide a precise look for the next six months to one year.

- **Agree on clear payment terms:** Establish clear payment terms from the beginning. This is very important for your business's future.

- **Invoice quickly:** Some aspects that influence cash flow are in the hands of a business, like when to raise an invoice. SMEs should raise invoice to clients as soon as the work is completed.

- **Make payments easy for customers:** The system of payments should be made as trouble-free as possible for your customer. Try to avoid payments by cheque and adopt the online mode of transfer.

- **Offer clients a fixed rate payment package:** One way that SMEs can guarantee good cash flow is by offering a periodic payment package.

- **Establishing payment arrangement that minimises debtor days:** Every business has the experience of developing a gap between invoicing and payment. In order to make this stable, try to establish direct debit as a business custom for collecting receipts.

- **Use technology to manage cash flow:** Technology can manage cash flow in a much easier manner. Cloud-based accounting saves time.

- **Do not focus on profit, focus on cash flow:** 90% of the SMEs do not have a cash flow plan from day one. If your cash flow is in order, your profit will be complemented.

- **Train an employee to monitor your cash flow:** Some small businesses assign a dedicated person to track the money going in and out. This makes the structure full proof.

- **Keep the bank informed: Banks can offer useful services like overdrafts or credit to businesses, particularly when they are starting out. Be in constant touch with your banker.**

It is true that different plans work for different businesses, and you should consult your accountant to see what works best for you. Circumstances change. When they do, your financial plan should change too.

STICK TO THE BASICS OF INVESTING

Turmoil in market causes investors to question their own decision and seek different approaches. But the only thing, investors who are investing in real estate, really need to do is follow some fundamental principles. One of the most important aspects you will ever need to lead a peaceful life is to know how to secure your financial well-being by investing in properties. One does not need to be a genius to do it. There are few basics to be followed, a plan to be formed and you should be ready to stick to it.

It can never be guaranteed that you will get rich from investments you make in real estate. But with an intelligent plan, you should be able to achieve financial security and enjoy the benefits.

- Diversify: It is better to put your eggs in different baskets than a single one. Buying a few shares of a number of real estate stocks cost more in commissions than putting all your money in one stock but eventually it pays off.
- Start investing early: The longer you have your money working for you, the more you will gain. If you are still in college and reading this, start saving now for making investments in real estate.
- Invest in things you know: Never invest in properties you can't illustrate with a crayon - goes an old saying. Put your money in real estate you have an idea about, be it commercial or any other type.

- Avoid fads: Past performance of a real estate stock is a bad predictor of results that may turn up in future days. Better do away with them.
- Don't let a market slump bring change to your long-term investment plan: Many a times, a slump in market has discouraged many people to make investments in real estate. However, those who had faith in their investments and held on gained in the end.
- Don't check the price of a property once you have sold it: After you've made a decision, stick with it. Look ahead, not behind.
- Don't panic: Bad times are inevitable, so are good times. Panic makes bad times a nightmare. It is better to fight it out and nullify the odds and wait for the brighter phase.
- Keep track of what is going on with your investments: No stocks, even real estate ones, are safe for a lifetime. Even the bluest blue chip can turn into a bad apple. Even if you are asleep, do so with your eyes open.
- Hold onto your winners and sell your losers: Sell the real estate stocks that are making you a loss. Don't wait to get even. But do guard the ones that are making you money.
- Stick to your plan: Never abandon your long-term plan because of losses. The market always goes up and down. Even when it is going up, you might not own the best performers.
- Be realistic about your tolerance for risk: If a big plunge is going to get to you, put a higher share of your portfolio in properties, land, value stocks or in cash.
- Get the best investment advice you can and then think for yourself: Do some research on your own rather than blindly following the tips and advises of brokers, analysts or even in the financial magazines when you are dealing with real estate and land.
- Avoid spending the principal: Set aside money for personal expenses. Never forget to reinvest the interest and dividends from your real estate stocks and bonds.

TIPS TO IDENTIFY A WRONG INVESTMENT

Investing in real estate is tricky like in any other investment. At times, you need to depend on others for information, but, in many cases, the information provided to you about lands, properties and real estate stocks may prove to be false or wrong. It is an utmost necessity to check things up and identify what the reality is. A wrong investment can lead to disaster and there are some ways it can be avoided.

Here are a few other ways to tell if you're getting the wrong type of investment advice.

- "Trust me. I got this."- If there is no explanation provided to you for how your money is being invested in properties, take it as a bad sign. Every bit of money you invest in properties should have a solid logic and turning a blind eye and hoping for the best isn't at all a good tactic.
- "Here's how we think you should play this."- A real estate investment plan should not consider how to play something, but how to plan for a wide range of eventualities. Trying to "play" on land types, commercial real estate or real estate stocks rarely work out very well. You would never dream of someone playing with your life savings.
- "We got a solid tip on this stock." - Acting on tips is not an option when you are dealing with real estate; it's just a way to lose your hard-earned money.

- "If you're not investing in so and so, you're missing out."- No one should ever recommend a real estate investment opportunity without taking into consideration your personal state of affairs. You should never receive a prescription without first being diagnosed.
- "We made 36 changes to your portfolio in the past six months to take advantage of market opportunities." - Making constant changes to your portfolio or strategy is a huge red flag.
- "Me, me, me, me." – You are not getting good real estate investment advice if no questions are being asked and the focus is only on the brokers, their past achievements or their firm.
- "It's a proprietary model." - You never want to invest in real estate with someone who cannot or will not explain how their strategy works. Real estate is something where one should be aware of everything.
- "We can guarantee stock-like returns with bond-like volatility, ensure you never have to touch your principal balance and avoid all losses on risky assets." - Guarantees make you feel secure. However, the maximum anyone can do is propose to give you a high probability for success. Nothing is ever a sure thing in the real estate related financial markets. Avoid those who constantly use the terms 'always' or 'never'.
- "We hedge out every risk you can think of." - Risk comes in many different forms especially when you are dealing with properties and there's no way to entirely nullify risk. Every real estate investment position involves some form of risk whether you recognize those risks or not.
- "I know that's what we told you we were going to do, but this time we're serious." Making errors in the property market will happen sometimes. Nobody is perfect. But the best way to moderate a financial situation will be how well they do what they said they were going to do at the outset.

CHAPTER 3

FUNDING YOUR INVESTMENT

Buyers and investors generally take help of a loan to pay for their real estate purchase. While banks used to offer one or two different types of loans to borrowers looking to buy a real estate property, things are a lot different now. Buyers can now borrow many different types of loans like home loan, industrial property loan, home extension loan, etc. to make sure that the loan product they choose perfectly suits their requirement.

And, it is not just the lenders who are looking to help the buyers, even developers now offer many different types of payment plans to make sure that purchasing a real estate property is not a financial burden on the buyers.

But with all the different types of loans and payment plans available, it is very important for buyers and investors to make sure that they clearly understand the advantages and drawbacks of everything available to them in order to protect themselves from making a mistake that can trouble them for years to come.

TYPES OF LOANS YOU CAN TAKE (INDUSTRIAL PROPERTY LOANS, RESIDENTIAL LOANS)

People who are looking to buy or invest in a real estate property can now take many different types of loans to pay for the purchase. However, apart from the standard loans, to buy a domestic or commercial property, lenders now offer many different types of loans to cater to the specific needs of the buyers.

The following are few of the most popular real estate loans available in India -

HOME LOANS

These are the most common type of loans and can be used to buy a new house or an old house. With a home loan, buyers can get up to 80-85% of the total cost of the house as loan which they can then repay in the form of EMIs.

 These home loans are offered along with floating or fixed interest rate. Almost all the banks and NBFCs offer this type of loan.

INDUSTRIAL PROPERTY LOANS

Buyers looking to buy a commercial property can do so with the help of industrial property loans. These loans are offered to owner-occupied properties as well as to investors. With this type of loan, buyers can get a loan of up to 80% of the total cost of the property and just like the home loans, these loans are also available with floating or fixed interest rate.

LAND PURCHASE LOANS

Land purchase loans can be taken by borrowers to purchase a plot of land where they can construct a residential property, commercial property or just purchase them for investment purposes. Majority of the banks offer land purchase loans and loans of up to 85% of the total cost of the land are provided by lenders.

HOME CONSTRUCTION LOANS

These type of loans are ideal for borrowers who want to construct a domestic or commercial property of their own and require funds for the construction purpose. However, the application and even the approval process of these loans are different from standard home and industrial property loans. The loan amount of a construction loan can be provided by the lender as a lump sum amount or in instalments on the basis of the construction progress.

EXPANSION OR EXTENSION LOANS

These type of loans are generally taken by home owners who want to expand their home. This expansion can include changes in current structure of the house for the purpose of adding extra space, like construction of a new floor, room, bigger washroom, etc. While majority of the banks offer loans for the above-mentioned purposes in the form of home expansion loans, some others offer them in the form of home improvement loans.

CONVERSION LOANS

The borrowers who have already purchased a house with the help of a home loan but now want to buy and entirely move to a new home can go for a conversion loan. With the help of these loans, the borrower will not be required to repay the loan of their previous property. However, these loans are known to be very expensive.

These are some of the most common types of loans one can take to buy or invest in a real estate property. Each of these different types of loans come with their own

 **advantages and disadvantages and thus, one should only make a decision after closely analyzing the different options.**

While lenders offer a variety of loan products to allow people to buy real estate properties, even the developers now offer a wide-range of payment plans to make things simpler for the buyers.

TYPES OF PAYMENT PLANS OFFERED BY BUILDERS

Purchasing a new home is supposed to be an exuberant experience. However, it is the financial burden that often hinders this experience preventing the buyers from enjoying their milestone. To minimize the financial burden and offer long term security of the finances, many of the developers have come up with unique payment plans. But before choosing any particular plan, it is very important to clearly understand the plan to make sure that they actually ease the burden and don't end up increasing it further.

Let us have a look at five of the most common payment plans offered by real estate developers -

1. DOWN-PAYMENT PLAN

A down-payment plan requires the buyer to pay about 10% while booking the property. From the remaining amount, around 80%-85% should be paid within 30 days from the date of booking and the remaining 5% to 10% is paid while taking the possession.

2. CONSTRUCTION-LINKED PAYMENT PLAN

Construction-linked payment plans require a buyer to pay 2-3 calendar-based instalments for the property and the remaining payment is linked to the progress of the construction. With such a plan, a buyer might pay 5% to 10% for booking a property, next 8% to 10% within a period of 3 months from the date of booking and next 15% to 20% within the next six months. Remaining amount will be paid in instalments when construction reaches pre-fixed milestones.

3. TIME-LINKED PAYMENT PLAN

Just like the above-mentioned construction-linked plan which is linked to the progress of construction, time-linked plan is time-bound. Irrespective of the progress of the construction, a buyer is required to pay fixed amount within fixed time frame. Even when there are delays in the construction plan, as per the contract, the buyer will be required to make the payment within the time frame.

4. FLEXI-PAYMENT PLAN

A flexi-payment plan is a combination of down-payment plan and construction-linked plan. It requires the buyer to pay about 10% while booking the property and about 30% from the remaining amount within a period of 30 days from the date of booking. 50% of the remaining amount is then paid in the form of instalments just like the construction-linked plan which is linked to the progress of the construction. And the last 10% is paid while taking the possession.

5. SUBVENTION PAYMENT PLAN

With a subvention payment plan, the buyer only pays 10% to 15% of the total cost of the property while purchasing it. The bank pays the remaining amount to the developer and a three-way agreement is created between the buyer, bank and developer. During the construction phase, developer pays interest for the buyer's loan to the bank. As the construction progresses, the bank disburses the loan amount to the developer. The EMI of the buyer only starts after the possession.

While these payment plans do make it easier for a buyer to buy a real estate property, each of them comes with their own share of advantages and disadvantages.

TAKING ADVANTAGE OF
SCHEMES AND OFFERS

With a variety of payment plans now available for the buyers, the financial burden that was once required to be carried by the buyer in the past while purchasing a property has substantially reduced. But are these plans really as good as they appear? Yes and No! The reality is that each of the payment plans comes with its advantages and risks, and thus, it is very important for a buyer to carefully weigh the ups and downs before choosing a plan.

Advantages and risks of the most popular plans are discussed below -

1. DOWN-PAYMENT PLAN
Down-payment plan was the only option available for the buyers in the past and it is still very popular. But just like other plans, it comes with advantages and risks too.

Advantages - A down-payment plan can provide the buyer with great discounts on property costs as the entire amount is paid to the developer upfront. Discounts of up to 10% can be gained by choosing this plan. Moreover, none of the other payment plans offer such a high discount.

Risks - These plans can prove very disadvantageous for the buyers if there are delays in the delivery or the construction of the project.

Moreover, there are also possibilities that the project can get abandoned because of some legal problems. And recovering money from the developer in such cases can be very difficult for the buyer.

2. CONSTRUCTION-LINKED PAYMENT PLAN

Also known as the Possession-Linked Plan, Construction-Linked Plan (CLP) is getting very popular among new buyers as the payment is linked with the progress of the construction. However, this type of plan can prove costly for the buyers.

Advantages - As the payment plan is not time-bound and is completely linked to the progress of the construction, the amount of risk for the buyers is very meagre. Moreover, with this type of plan even the developer tries to complete the project on time to ensure a consistent cash flow.

Risks - CLPs cost much more to the buyers if the total amount of interest paid to the lender is taken into consideration as the loan tenure is generally longer. The repayment of the principal amount begins after the possession and only interest is paid during the entire construction phase.

3. TIME-LINKED PAYMENT PLAN

As the buyer is required to pay instalments even in case of delays, time-linked payment plan is not very popular among buyers.

Advantages - With a time-linked payment plan, the developer might provide discounts of about 8% to 10% as the buyer will be required to pay the instalments irrespective of the progress of the construction. Other than that, such plans do not provide any other kind of advantages.

Risks - As per the contract, the buyer will be required to pay the instalments even if there are delays. When payments are not made on time, the developer has the right to charge penalties too. However, this type of plan is still not as risky as a down-payment plan as the entire amount is not paid up front.

4. FLEXI-PAYMENT PLAN

Flexi-payment plans are highly popular with new launches and projects and the buyer is required to pay about 40% of the total cost of the property within a month or so.

Advantages - As about 40% is paid by the buyer within a month of booking the property, developers generally give a discount of about 5% to 8%.

Risks - Delays and abandoning of projects are very common with new launches. With this type of plan, it can be difficult for the buyer to recover money from the developer if the project is hit due to some reason. Moreover, if this plan is compared with a CLP, the buyer is required to pay interest of about 40% to 50% of the total cost of the project right from the first year after booking, whereas, with a CLP, interest of about 30% to 35% of the total cost of the property is paid in the first year. So, to an extent, CLPs are cheaper than flexi-payment plans.

5. SUBVENTION PAYMENT PLAN

While subvention plans look too tempting and many developers offer different types of subvention plans, they too come with their share of advantages and risks.

Advantages - The buyer is only required to pay 10% to 15% of the total cost of the property initially and he gets adequate time until possession to arrange the funds which are then paid through EMIs.

Risks - As the developer is required to pay the EMI to the lender throughout the construction process on the behalf of the buyer, if at all the developer fails to pay the EMI on time, it is the credit rating of the buyer that gets negatively affected.

SO, HOW TO CHOOSE A PAYMENT PLAN?

As all the different payment plans come with their advantages and risks, it is the available funds and personal situation of a buyer that can help them decide the payment plan.

 **If a buyer is taking a home loan, lenders only disburse the loan amount as per the construction progress and in such a scenario, a CLP is what a buyer would require. Moreover, CLPs are also great while dealing with a new developer or one who doesn't have a very impressive track record.**

If the financial condition of the buyer allows them to provide down payment or if they have confidence in the credibility of the developer, down-payment option can be great to get substantial discount on the cost of the property. However, delays are very common in the current market scenario and thus, people generally go for CLPs even if they are required to pay more interest. And if the buyer is taking a loan to purchase, knowing one's loan-bearing ability should also be taken into consideration.

HOW MUCH LOAN BURDEN CAN YOU TAKE?

Once a buyer has chosen the lender from which he/she will take the home loan and the dotted line is signed, it doesn't take very long before the buyer moves into the new house with their family and starts repaying the loan through EMI. While things do look pretty well in the first few months, over time, the buyer realizes that they failed to consider the household expenses or considered them to be much lower than they actually are.

School fees of children, social life, annual holidays, entertainment bills, restaurant bills, unexpected legal or medical expenses, etc. are some of the aspects that buyers generally fail to consider while taking a home loan and choosing a repayment plan. And before the buyer gets to know it, the monthly EMIs turn into a much bigger burden than expected.

 This is a very common scenario which many home loan borrowers go through. People generally realize at a later stage that they have bit a lot more than they can actually chew.

So, before taking a home loan, it is very important to first understand how much loan burden one can carry. And the below mentioned tips can help buyers make a better decision.

1. DEBT-TO-INCOME RATIO

The debt-to-income ratio is one of the best indicators of how much loan burden one can take. This ratio is a fraction of the monthly income of the borrower and how much EMI he/she will pay every month. In India, majority of the home loan borrowers generally pay 30% to 40% of their income every month as EMI. However, experts generally recommend that the ratio should be less than 30%. Borrowers with higher monthly income can easily pay more.

2. LIFESTYLE

Another important factor while determining how much loan burden a borrower can take is the lifestyle of the borrower. If the borrower along with his/her family likes to dine at expensive restaurants on a frequent basis or if one's children go to expensive schools, they might not be able to pay a major part from their monthly salary as EMI even when their salary is significantly higher as compared to the EMI amount. Moreover, borrowers who do not have a stable job should also take this as a factor. Delayed payments or non-payment of the EMIs can lead to additional penalties which can sometimes be very high.

3. INTEREST RATE

Another important factor is the interest rate on the home loan. If interest rates are about to rise in future, it is important to try and do everything possible to reduce the loan tenure. On the other hand, if the interest rates are supposed to fall in future, it will be much easier for the borrower to repay higher amount on a longer time frame. Also, female home buyers can get higher loan amount and many lenders keep interest rate for female borrowers lower than the standard rates.

These are three of the most important factors that can allow a buyer to understand how much home loan burden one can carry. As home loans are long-term commitments, it is very important to take decisions in the wisest possible manner to make sure that the repayment is done in a timely manner.

CHAPTER 4

KNOWING THINGS IN ADVANCE

Just like any other investment, investing in real estate also requires you to know a number of things in advance. While thoroughly knowing about the local markets, browsing through multiple options, etc. are some of the things that are very important, there are many other things that should be known even before you start searching for a property.

For instance, you should first have a clear idea about your investment needs. While real estate investments are generally thought of as a type of long-term investment, there are many investors who make money even by investing in them for short- or medium-term. Apart from this, do you know what negative cash flow is and how it can affect your investment? Or what are the real estate policies and laws in India?

Also, what are your thoughts about investing in a real estate property in a foreign country? While investing in a real estate property does carry a lot of potential, the potential is only as good as your understanding of this sector and your decision-making abilities. Hopefully, this section will answer a lot of your queries regarding the matters discussed above.

IDENTIFYING YOUR INVESTMENT NEEDS (SHORT-TERM, MID-TERM, LONG-TERM)

Every investor has his/her own goals when it comes to investing in real estate properties. While majority of the investors think of it as a long-term investment, there are many who invest with short-term and mid-term goals in mind. But if you are unable to identify your investment needs, perhaps a detailed analysis of these investment durations might provide you with a better idea.

SHORT- OR MID-TERM REAL ESTATE INVESTMENT

The main idea behind flipping or wholesaling a real estate property is to increase your net worth/cash reserve substantially in a short span of time. For instance, if an investor is able to flip a property every two months while keeping about Rs. 1 lakh as profit in every deal, in a year the investor can make around Rs. 6 lakhs. However, this amount can be substantially higher if the investor has the expertise required to find amazing deals. As a result, beginners are often recommended to not get emotionally attached to their property if they are looking for short-term or medium-term gains.

> Basically, it is just a number game that has been made complicated by the investors. If the numbers are not working in your favour for a particular property, avoid accepting reduced profit (less than Rs. 1 lakh) and look for a better deal.

However, expertise also plays a very important role in the entire process. Better the knowledge about real estate properties in India, higher are the chances of gaining great returns. So, only enter the real estate market with a short-term or mid-term goal in mind when you are sure about what you are doing or when you have someone experienced to guide you through the process.

LONG-TERM REAL ESTATE INVESTMENT

If an investor is looking for financial independence, long-term real estate investment has all the right ingredients for the same. Rent and capital appreciation are the two different ways through which a long-term investor can earn money. However, an investor should be financially ready to accept such a big responsibility. It is generally recommended that an investor should have around Rs. 10 lakhs as cash reserve even after buying the property. Apart from this, disposable income to keep up with the property expenses irrespective of whether or not there is a renter living in the property is also important.

Long-term real estate investment is actually an excellent way to earn passive income and build wealth. While it is somewhat easier than short- and mid-term real estate investment, due diligence is highly recommended while buying a property.

Choosing investment is all about the financial goals of an investor. While real estate investments carry excellent potential, it is also very important to be careful about every single step to ensure maximum returns and protect yourself from negative cash flow.

WHAT IS NEGATIVE CASH FLOW? WHY IS THERE NO POSITIVE CASH FLOW INVESTMENT IN INDIA?

A company uses cash to pay its bills. The flow of cash or the cash flow can be in variety of forms, like checks, card payments, wire transfers, etc. Investing, operating and financing are three important areas on which the cash flow of a company depends. And this flow can be both in and out of the company account. Cash flow fluctuates within an accounting period which can be a year, quarter or a month and can be negative as well as positive.

 **Negative cash flow is when the outflow of cash is more than the inflow within a specific period of time. However, this doesn't really mean that the company is suffering from losses as this can be due to a mismatch in the income and expenditure.**

Similarly, in the real estate investment a negative cash flow is said to take place when the investor spends more than he/she is earning within a specific period of time. Once the property is purchased, EMI, taxes, repairs, vacancy if it is a buy-to-let property, etc. are the reasons that can require the investor to spend more money. And when the rent or the capital appreciation is not as much as these additional costs, it is termed as a negative cash flow investment. And the main reason for this negative cash flow in real estate investment is the increasing cost of properties.

COST OF PROPERTY AND NEGATIVE CASH FLOW

The poor economic condition of the country affected several sectors, including the real estate sector. Escalating prices and piling inventory have reduced the demand across all the classes of real estate assets.

In the past, people generally entered into the real estate market when they were looking to buy a home for themselves. Over time, the buyer invested in a second property and either shifted to the new property to let out the first property on rent or used to let out the new purchase to earn monthly passive income. Negative cash flow was not really a matter of concern as capital appreciation was substantial in the past. Majority of the real estate investors used this formula and actually succeeded. But past is past.

While the outlook for future is positive, the current scenario is not too impressive. The appreciation levels are low and the prices of properties are still increasing. As a result, be it capital appreciation or earning through monthly rent, the risk of negative cash flow is at its peak.

But this doesn't really make real estate investment a bad idea. At the most, the investor might be required to add some extra money to the rent they receive to repay their loan and the capital appreciation might not be as good as it used to be in the past.

As a matter of fact, many Indian investors are now investing in foreign countries to earn better returns.

WHY SHOULD YOU ALSO CONSIDER INVESTING ABROAD?

With the increasing globalization, savvy real estate investors from India are now investing in foreign countries to diversify their portfolio and to get better returns on their investments. With the sluggish growth of the real estate sector in India and the RBI increasing the foreign remittance limit up to $250,000 from $125,000, many of the investors believe that now is the right time to invest in the real estate properties in foreign countries.

Let us look at some reasons that make real estate investments in foreign countries an excellent choice for investors -

DIVERSIFICATION

Needless to say, the main benefit of investing in a foreign country is to diversify the portfolio. While the real estate sector is somewhat stagnant at the moment in India, things are pretty stable in the real estate sector of many other foreign countries, like Dubai, Singapore, Mauritius, Malaysia, and the like. As a result, by diversifying the portfolio and buying real estate properties in foreign countries, an investor can take advantage of the stable real estate scenario of other countries.

PASSIVE INCOME

 Just like investment in India, passive income is a major advantage of investing in real estate properties in foreign countries.

You can let out the property on rent and the rent paid by renters in a lot of countries is much better as compared to the rent an investor receives in India. The best thing is that an investor can easily hire a management company to look after their property. Right from the maintenance, repairs, to rent collection, these agencies will take care of everything.

While there are several advantages of investing in foreign countries, a lot of people in India still believe that it is the Indian real estate market that is more promising. They believe that the current real estate scenario in India is highly favourable and investors should think twice before making an investment in a foreign country as they can lose an amazing opportunity.

 However, increasing number of Indians are already buying properties in foreign countries and this is pretty evident from the numbers.

In the year 2015, Indian investors made a total of 4,089 real estate transactions in Dubai alone worth around Rs. 23,000 crores. Moreover, as per a report from the US National Association of Realtors, Indians spent a total of $5.8 billion in buying real estate properties in the US between 2013 and 2014 which is about 6% more than the previous year.

While there is no denying that things do look promising for the Indian real estate sector in future, it is something that will happen in future. On the other hand, the investors investing in real estate properties in foreign countries are already earning handsome returns on their investment. While the decision is up to you, if you actually do plan to invest in a foreign country make sure that you do it carefully.

WHAT YOU NEED TO KNOW IF INVESTING ABROAD?

The trend of investing in real estate properties in foreign countries is rising among Indian investors. But as an investor, especially ones who are investing for the first time, they should do so very carefully to make sure that their investment is actually in a position to provide them with the desired results.

Investors looking to invest abroad should definitely keep the below mentioned points in mind before making any decision -

LIBERALIZED REMITTANCE SCHEME (LRS)
Under the Liberalized Remittance Scheme, RBI now allows remittance of up to $250,000 in a year for any purpose. However, there are some exceptions to the law. Moreover, an investor can also go for joint property as this can allow the co-applicant to remit the same amount in a year. Also, there is no limit on the number or frequency of the remittance within this limit of $250,000, allowing investors to buy properties in foreign countries for which they need to make the payments in instalments.

SALE PROCEEDS AND RENT
An investor who has invested in a real estate property in a foreign country is required to transfer the rental income or the sale proceeds

when the investor exits the investment to an Indian bank account within 90 days from when the rent is paid or the property is sold.

INCOME TAX IMPLICATIONS

There can be many different tax complexities, especially if apart from India, the country in which an investor invests also levies taxes on the earnings from the property. Moreover, as per the exchange regulations of the foreign country, there can be limitations for the repatriation of the proceeds from the sale of the property when the investor sells it. In India, the rental income from the property in a foreign country is taxable just like the second property rental income from an Indian property.

However, if the purchase is supported with the help of a certificate, the interest that is paid on the loan taken in foreign country for purchasing a property is deductible. However, there are some exceptions too. If the loan is not taken from particular Indian banks for purchasing a property abroad, the principal repayment amount of the loan is not deductible.

Moreover, under DTAA (Double Taxation Avoidance Agreement) of India and the other country, investors can protect themselves from paying the tax twice. And even if India doesn't have a DTAA with the foreign country, investors can still take advantage of the foreign tax credit if they have all the required documents, like income tax that is paid overseas, tax return filed overseas, etc.

Properties that are held for more than three years in a foreign country before selling will be taxed as long term capital gain which is 20% after applying the indexation benefit. And properties that are sold before three years are taxed according to the investor's income tax slab rate.

The long term capital gains can be exempted if the investor invests the sale proceeds in a residential property in India or the NHAI/REC bonds specified by the government. However, this exemption is subject to a variety of additional conditions. Apart from these, irrespective of whether an investor is investing in India or abroad, there are other important laws and policies related to real estate that an investor should know.

REAL ESTATE LAWS AND POLICIES IN INDIA YOU SHOULD KNOW

With Foreign Direct Investment Act of 2005, not just Indians, but investors from all over the world are now interested in buying real estate property in India. However, majority of the investors often struggle with the problem of lack of clarity with regards to the laws and policies related to the real estate sector.

The below mentioned list of some very important laws and policies related to real estate can be very helpful for investors who are now investing in the real estate market or have plans to do so in future.

LAWS AND POLICIES FOR REAL ESTATE IN INDIA
The Central Acts, FDI Policy of 2010, Regulation and Development Act of 2016, and the local municipal laws are some of the most important norms which govern the real estate sector in India. Purchase, sale, lease or loan, everything related to real estate is governed by these laws and policies.

Some of the most important sections of these laws and policies are -

COMPETENT TO CONTRACT
As per Section 11 of the Control Act, an individual who is looking to purchase a real estate property should be competent to contract. This means that he/she should be -

- Above 18 years
- Not prohibited under any Indian law
- Of sane mind

If an individual is competent to contract, he/she can buy or invest in immovable property in India.

TITLE CHECK

As per the Registration Act of 1908, every written document which creates interest or transfers interest in any immovable property and whose value is more than Rs. 100 should be compulsorily registered in land registry. These documents are deeds which indicate the title to immovable property and can be lease deeds, sale deeds, or mortgage deeds.

TRANSFER OF PROPERTY

Any kind of real estate transaction, like sale, mortgage, or lease is governed by the Transfer of Property Act. The transactions are brought into effect with the help of written documents that can transfer an interest or the entire interest to transferee.

FDI POLICY

A non-resident is not allowed to purchase immovable property in India. However, they can invest in an Indian company that is involved in real estate development as per the FDI Policy. They can do so with the help of the automatic route and are not required to seek any kind of approval for the same from RBI, Ministry of Commerce, or The Department of Industrial Policy and Promotion. But once the inward remittance is done or the investor is issued shares of a real estate development company, they are required to inform this to RBI within 30 days.

While there are many other real estate laws and policies that an investor or buyer should know, the ones mentioned above are some of the most important ones.

Growing NRI population and its impact on the Real Estate Sector

01

The Reserve Bank of India has considerably eased investment norms by NRIs/PIOs who want to invest in real estate. They can buy, sell, gift and inherit immovable property. However, the prohibited categories include agricultural land, plantation property and farmhouses.

02

An NRI/PIO may remit an amount, not exceeding US $1 million per financial year out of the balances held in NRO accounts. However, the repatriation is subject to production of documentary evidence in support of acquisition, inheritance or legacy of assets and payment of applicable taxes in India.

03

Residents can now remit home loan EMI for NRIs.

04

On the taxation front, wealth-tax has been abolished. On the capital gains received while selling immovable property, the cost inflation index will enable NRIs to minimize tax liability.

REIT LISTING IN INDIA

1

In the last two budgets, the Central Government has worked on easing the path for REIT listing in India. It has done so by providing pass-through status for rental income and has rationalized capital gains for the sponsors in different conditions.

HOUSING NEEDS OF THE POOR

In order to address the housing needs of the poor, housing activity under the PradhanMantriAwas Yojna, has been implemented by this government and the Finance Minister has proposed to give 100% deduction for profits to undertakings from housing project for flats up to a certain area in four metro cities and other certain areas in other cities.

2

TAX

MINIMUM ALTERNATE TAX

3

In order to address the housing needs of the poor, housing activity under the Pradhan MantriAwasYojna, has been implemented by this government and the Finance Minister has proposed to give 100% deduction for profits to undertakings from housing project for flats up to a certain area in four metro cities and other certain areas in other cities.

MAJOR BOOST FOR REAL ESTATE SECTOR DURING THE LAST TWO YEARS

1 SMART CITY

The Proposal: With a vision to bring a new horizon of urban growth, the Government has proposed to build 100 smart cities in India. A list of 98 cities has been declared out of which 33 cities have been already chosen over two rounds. The Government has so far allocated around Rs 48,000 crores as seed funding.

HOUSING FOR ALL BY 2022   2

The present Government has proposed to build houses for all the people belonging to the Economically Weaker Section (EWS) & Lower Income Group (LIG) who does not have houses.. The initiative will provide interest subsidies and financial aid and has the vision to build around 110 million individual units by 2022.

3 REITS: ENABLING RETAIL INVESTMENT IN THE INDIAN COMMERCIAL SECTOR

Through Real Estate Investment Trust small investors are able to invest into income generating commercial real estate units. The Government has been taking policy-based initiatives to expedite the process for implementing REITs in the Indian market.

REAL ESTATE REGULATORY ACT   4

With the objective of bringing transparency into the overall Indian real estate industry, the present Government has brought a proposal for a string of regulations in the form of a new law, the Real Estate Regulation Act. The Act will make it mandatory for the developer to share all the relevant information regarding projects with the Real Estate Regulatory Act (RERA).

Curbing of Black Money Flow and its Impact

Steps taken by the GOI and its impacts are:

IMPARTING SKILLS TO THE MANPOWER FOR EFFECTIVE ACTION:

As a part of capacity building and skill development, many senior officers have sent abroad for specialized training in the field of International Taxation and Transfer Pricing.

JOINING THE GLOBAL CRUSADE AGAINST BLACK MONEY:

Global effort are being made against curbing black money and India is playing proactive part in pointing out paucities in the assessment of various countries through the Peer Review Group of the Global Forum.

DEVELOPING SYSTEMS FOR IMPLEMENTATION:

The strength of Foreign Tax Division has been doubled to deal with proper exchange of information.

CREATING AN APPROPRIATE LEGISLATIVE FRAMEWORK:

The Government of India is on a path to strengthen the legislative frame work so that the generation of black money in the country could be controlled along with flight of illicit fund to tax-heavens.

DIRECTORATE OF INCOME TAX:

The creation of the Directorate of Income Tax (Criminal Investigation), in the Central Board of Direct Taxes has also been approved by the Government. The DCI will take up criminal matters which may have financial implication punishable as an offence under any direct tax law.

SETTING UP INSTITUTIONS FOR DEALING WITH ILLICIT FUNDS:

An Exchange of Information (EoI) Cell is being set up by the Government of India so that effective exchange of information may be made possible in order to curb tax evasion. The cell is to be placed under Foreign Tax Division of CBDT.

Types of Payment Plans Offered by Builders

Let us have a look at 5 of the most common payment plans offered by real estate developers-

01 Down-Payment Plan

A buyer is required to pay fixed amount within fixed time frame. Even when there are delays in the construction plan, as per the contract, the buyer will be required to make the payment within the time frame.

02 Construction-Linked Payment Plan

With such a plan, a buyer might pay 5% to 10% for booking a property, next 8% to 10% within a period of 3 months from the date of booking and next 15% to 20% within the next 6 months. Remaining amount will be paid in instalments when construction reaches pre-fixed milestones.

03 Time-Linked Payment Plan

A buyer is required to pay fixed amount within fixed time frame. Even when there are delays in the construction plan, as per the contract, the buyer will be required to make the payment within the time frame

04 Flexi-Payment Plan

It requires the buyer to pay about 10% while booking the property and about 30% from the remaining amount within a period of 30 days from the date of booking. 50% of the remaining amount is then paid in the form of instalments . The last 10% is paid while taking possession.

05 Subvention Payment Plan

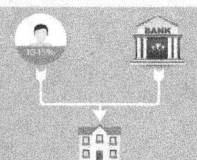

With a subvention payment plan, the buyer only pays 10% to 15% of the total cost of the property while purchasing it. The bank pays the remaining amount to the developer and a 3-way agreement is created between the buyer, bank and developer.

How Much Loan Burden Can You Take?

Before taking a home loan, it is very important to first understand how much loan burden one can carry. And the below mentioned tips can help buyers make a better decision.

Debt-to-Income Ratio

The debt-to-income ratio is one of the best indicators of how much loan burden one can take. This ratio is a fraction of the monthly income of the borrower and how much EMI he/she will pay every

Lifestyle

Another important factor while determining how much loan burden a borrower can take is the lifestyle of the borrower.

Interest Rate

Another important factor is the interest rate on the home loan. If interest rates are about to rise in future, it is important to try and do everything possible to reduce the loan tenure. On the other hand, if the interest rates are supposed to fall in future, it will be much easier for the borrower to repay higher amount on a longer time frame.

REAL ESTATE LAWS AND POLICIES IN INDIA YOU SHOULD KNOW

(The below mentioned list of some very important laws and policies related to real estate can be very helpful for investors who are now investing in the real estate market or have plans to do so in future)

LAWS AND POLICIES FOR REAL ESTATE IN INDIA

It is the Central Acts, FDI Policy of 2010, Regulation and Development Act of 2016, and the local municipal laws are some of the most important norms which govern the real estate sector in India. Purchase, sale, lease or loan, everything related to real estate is governed by these laws and policies.

Some of the most important sections of these laws and policies are-

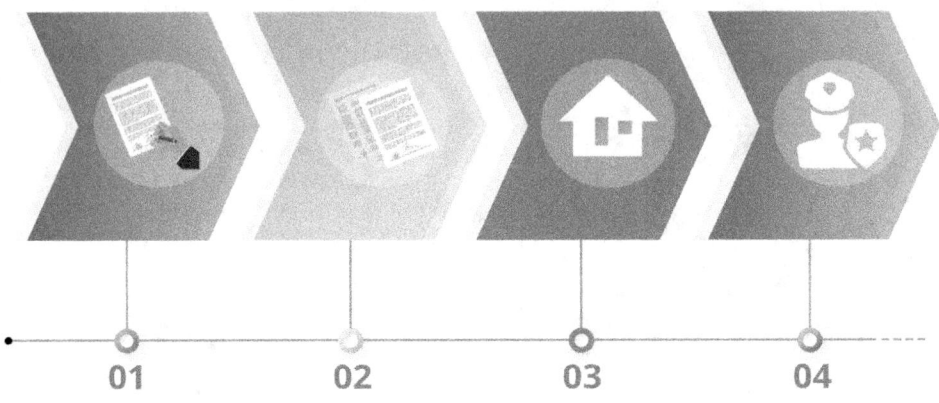

01	02	03	04
COMPETENT TO CONTRACT	**TITLE CHECK**	**TRANSFER OF PROPERTY**	**FDI POLICY**

COMPETENT TO CONTRACT

As per Section 11 of the Control Act, an individual who is looking to purchase a real estate property should be competent to contract. This means that he/she should be-

Above 18 years
● Not prohibited under any Indian law
● Of sane mind

If an individual is competent to contract, he/she can buy or invest in immovable property in India

TITLE CHECK

As per the Registration Act of 1908, every written document which creates interest or transfers interest in any immovable property and whose value is more than Rs. 100 should be compulsorily registered in land registry. These documents are deeds which indicate the title to immovable property and can be lease deeds, sale deeds, or mortgage deeds.

TRANSFER OF PROPERTY

Any kind of real estate transaction, like sale, mortgage, or lease is governed by the Transfer of Property Act. The transactions are brought into effect with the help of written documents that can transfer an interest or the entire interest to transferee.

FDI POLICY

A non-resident is not allowed to purchase immovable property in India. However, they can invest in an Indian company that is involved in real estate development as per the FDI Policy. They can do so with the help of the automatic route and are not required to seek any kind of approval for the same from RBI, Ministry of Commerce, or The Department of Industrial Policy and Promotion.

Documents You Should Have When Applying for a Loan

The documents are divided in three different categories- General Documents, Income Documents for Salaried and Non-Salaried Borrowers and Property Documents.

GENERAL DOCUMENTS

- Duly-filled home loan application
- 3-5 passport size photographs
- Government-approved ID proof, like Passport, PAN Card, Aadhar Card, Driving License, etc.
- Residence proof, like Telephone Bill, Electricity Bill, Passport, etc.
  Business address proof for non-salaried borrowers
- Bank account statement of about 6 months
  Statement of personal liabilities and assets
  Identification of signature from bankers

INCOME DOCUMENTS

Salaried Borrowers-
Apart from these, a salaried borrower will also be required to submit any one of the following-

- Letter from their employer
- Form 16
- Promotion or increment letter
- Pay slip of last 2 months
- Income tax returns of at least 3 years

NON-SALARIED BORROWERS

Along with the above mentioned general documents, a non-salaried borrower will also be required to provide-

- Small introduction of their business or profession
- Copy of the Registration Certificate of their establishment
- Copy of Registration Certificate for deducting Profession Tax
- Certificate of Practice
- Investment proof
- Advance tax receipts if any
- Apart from these, they also need to submit any one of the following-
- Chartered Accountant attested Profit and Loss Statement along with Balance Sheet of last 2 years of the company
- Income tax returns of at least 3 years

PROPERTY DOCUMENTS

- Original Agreement of Sale, Sale Deed
- Paid receipts of building and land tax
- Revenue authority certified location sketch of property
- Possession certificate
- Original receipts of the payments that are made for the flat in advance

OTHER DOCUMENTS

- If the borrower is taking a loan to purchase a plot of land, the borrower also needs to submit a declaration agreeing to the construction of house on that land within a fixed amount of time
- Report from a lawyer as per the instructions from the bank
- Valuation report from a professional and legal individual.

CHAPTER 5

DOCUMENTS

Investing in a real estate property to earn handsome returns or buying a first home is nothing short of a dream come true for a lot of us. However, in the current real estate scenario it might not take much time for this dream to transform in a nightmare. The famous Campa Cola Compound in Mumbai is a perfect example of this predicament.

While there is no denying the fact that the price, location and date of possession are some of the most important aspects that a buyer should look out for while searching for a real estate property, it is also very important to protect yourself from a fraudulent real estate transaction. And one of the most important things that you must look out for is the legal documents related to the property.

There are many different documents that a potential buyer should thoroughly inspect to ensure that the property they are about to buy is completely legal. Apart from the documents, physical inspection of the property, especially if it is a resale property, is highly important too. Professional help in these matters is highly recommended and can actually protect a buyer from making a wrong decision.

DOCUMENTS YOU SHOULD HAVE WHEN APPLYING FOR A LOAN

Investors looking for a home loan or an industrial property loan will be required to provide the bank or financial institution with a variety of documents. While the document requirement is almost similar across all the banks and NBFCs, there can be slight differences on the basis of the specific requirements.

The documents are divided in three different categories - General Documents, Income Documents for Salaried and Non-Salaried Borrowers and Property Documents.

GENERAL DOCUMENTS
- Duly-filled home loan application
- 3-5 passport size photographs
- Government-approved ID proof, like Passport, PAN Card, Aadhar Card, Driving License, etc.
- Residence proof, like Telephone Bill, Electricity Bill, Passport, etc.
- Business address proof for non-salaried borrowers
- Bank account statement of about six months
- Statement of personal liabilities and assets
- Identification of signature from bankers

INCOME DOCUMENTS

SALARIED BORROWERS-
Apart from these, a salaried borrower will also be required to submit any one of the following-

- Letter from their employer
- Form 16
- Promotion or increment letter
- Pay slip of last two months
- Income tax returns of at least three years

NON-SALARIED BORROWERS-
Along with the above mentioned general documents, a non-salaried borrower will also be required to provide-

- Small introduction of their business or profession
- Copy of the Registration Certificate of their establishment
- Copy of the Registration Certificate for deducting Professional Tax
- Certificate of Practice
- Investment proof
- Advance tax receipts if any

APART FROM THESE, THEY ALSO NEED TO SUBMIT ANY ONE OF THE FOLLOWING-
- Chartered Accountant attested Profit and Loss Statement along with Balance Sheet of last two years of the company
- Income tax returns of at least three years

PROPERTY DOCUMENTS
- Original Agreement of Sale, Sale Deed
- Paid receipts of building and land tax
- Revenue authority certified location sketch of property
- Possession certificate
- Original receipts of the payments that are made for the flat in advance

- Copy of approved building plan
- Detailed estimate of the total cost of the house or construction
- Original NOC from builder or housing society
- Letter from housing board, society or builder with their bank account number and other banking details for remitting the instalments of the purchase

OTHER DOCUMENTS

- If the borrower is taking a loan to purchase a plot of land, the borrower also needs to submit a declaration agreeing to the construction of house on that land within a fixed period of time
- Report from a lawyer as per the instructions from the bank
- Valuation report from a professional and legal individual.

Be it a home loan or industrial property loan, these are the documents that a borrower will be required to submit for successful approval of their loan.

DOCUMENTS TO HAVE AS A BUYER

Real estate transactions in India are highly document intensive because of the complex regulatory, statutory and legal framework. Research suggests that about 80% of the buyers do not get all the property documents while purchasing a property. Without all the legal documents in place, a buyer can face legal problems at a later stage, especially while trying to sell the property.

Every buyer should have the below-mentioned documents -

TITLE DEED/SALE DEED/CONVEYANCE DEED/MOTHER DEED

A sale deed is the most important piece of document which works as an evidence for the transfer of ownership to the buyer from seller. Moreover, it is also the main document with the help of which a buyer can then sell the property to another buyer.

KHATA CERTIFICATE AND EXTRACTS

Khata means account and *Khata* Certificate is required to register new property and to transfer ownership of a property. The *Khata* Certificate can be obtained from Assistant Revenue Officer of the area and should clearly mention the name of the owner.

Khata Extract is for the purpose of seeking details from the assessment register. It is required for buying a property or to get trading license.

RTC EXTRACTS

RTC Extract contains all the details of the land, including the present and past owner of the land, their holdings, name of tenants, charges that are levied on the property, land status, etc. This is issued by the Village Accountant and is required for establishing the Title of Land if the property is located on a land that is converted.

GENERAL POWER OF ATTORNEY

This is a legal document which provides a person with the right to act on someone else's behalf as their legal representative and make financial and legal decisions, including sale of the property, on their behalf. It is required to ensure that the previous purchase or sale was carried by a person who was authorized by the original buyer or seller.

SANCTIONING OF BUILDING PLAN BY STATUTORY AUTHORITY

The approval of building plan helps to ensure that the property is built according to specific rules and regulations. It establishes the fact that the property is actually authorized and its construction is legal.

NOC

Before beginning with the construction, a developer is required to take NOC from around 19 government departments, like Fire and Safety Department, Pollution Control Board, etc. A buyer should ask for copies of all the different NOCs before buying a property.

While there are many other documents that a buyer should have, the ones mentioned above are the most important ones. Moreover, there are some states in India that require additional documents. So, make sure that you search about all the different documents and have them in place to protect yourself from legal troubles in future.

INSPECTION OF PROPERTY BEFORE SIGNING A DEAL

After thoroughly researching the market, local property rates, etc. when a buyer is finally ready to invest in a particular real estate property, a thorough inspection of the property, especially a resale property, is very important. Just like every other form of investment, buying residential or commercial property is risky. However, this risk can be substantially reduced if not eliminated completely by taking some time out to inspect the physical condition of the property. If a buyer fails to inspect the property on their own or hire a professional to do the job before buying, it can lead to costly repairs in future.

Some of the most important things that a buyer should definitely check during an inspection include -

WALLS THAT BACK BATHROOMS

While inspecting the house, make sure that the walls that back the bathrooms are thoroughly inspected for signs of water leaks or moisture penetration. While this is not a type of structural defect, these penetrations and leaks can grow over time and can require the buyers to make substantial investments in the repair.

CEILINGS

Look at all the ceilings to make sure that they are fixed firmly in place and are not sagging or have a parachute-like appearance. Buyers can check this easily by shining torch across all the ceilings as it will show all the defects and deflections in the ceiling. The ceiling corners should also be checked for signs of water penetration.

MOULD IN BEDROOM OR BATHROOM

If they have been cleaned recently, moulds can look like dirty patches on ceilings and walls. A buyer will be required to hire a professional remediation company to remove the mould and this can be an expensive affair. Apart from cleaning it, it is also very important to find out the root cause of mould. Is it just due to poor upkeep or there are other reasons involved? Try to find out before signing the deal.

CRACKS ON WALLS

External as well as internal walls should be visually checked for large cracks. Cracks that have properties of cracking excessively or the ones that have a width of more than 1.5mm can be a major cause of concern and it is highly recommended that such cracks be inspected by professional property inspectors.

WALL PLASTERING

The plastering on the internal walls can be inspected for hairline cracks which are also known as map cracks because they look similar to a map. These types of cracks are generally an outcome of incorrect plaster application during construction. If these cracks are found at one location, there is a major possibility that they will be present elsewhere as well. These cracks can continue to develop further and can also get loose when paintings or other wall fixings are installed.

If a buyer is unsure about this entire inspection process, it is better to hire a professional property inspector to do the job. While this will certainly require the buyer to spend some money, a professional inspector can actually save lots of money and can protect buyers from making a wrong decision.

HOW TO CHECK THE DOCUMENTS OF A PROPERTY

Increasing number of new property buyers are now facing litigations due to their purchase. As a result, it is very important to make sure that the property you purchase is completely legal even if the project is from a reputable developer or company.

Apart from the litigations related to the property, these problems also increase the burden for owners who take home loans or live on rent. This is because majority of the property-related cases in court generally run for years and even when the court's verdict is in the favour of the buyers, the developer has the right to appeal again and stretch the matter further.

To make sure that the real estate transaction is free from litigations, there are a few factors that an investor can keep in mind.

TITLE DEED AND *KHATA*
While there are a number of documents that an investor should verify before making a purchase, Title Deed and *Khata* are two of the most important ones. Investor can look for records related to the Title Deed of a property at sub-registrar's office. The report will encompass all the important information about the owner of the property as well as the modifications in the title.

Khata is a document which supports title and should have a mention of the current owner of the property. The *Khata* document can be verified with the records of the local municipal body. It is very important to make sure that the present owner's entry is available in the *Khata* document as it will be required for getting electricity approval, loan, etc.

PROJECT PLAN

If it is an under-construction project, one can check the building plan to ensure that it is sanctioned by concerned authorities. This can be done by comparing the actual built-up of the project with the sanctioned plan to avoid investing in properties that are constructed illegally.

LEGAL DUES

The Encumbrance Certificate can be inspected to make sure that the property is free from any kind of mortgages or legal dues. If it is a housing society, NOC (No-Objection Certificate) can also help an **investor to check whether or not the property is legal.**

BANK APPROVAL

An excellent way to make sure whether or not a property is legal is a bank approval. Banks only approve loans for properties that are legal and have all the necessary documents. The bank will check the title clearances as well as all the other documents which can help the buyer ascertain that the property is actually legal and safe for investment.

If an investor is unaware of the documents which they should check before buying a property, hiring a professional for this job can be an excellent option.

PART 3

BUILDING YOUR RENTAL INCOME

CAPITAL APPRECIATION OR INCOME FROM RENT

Profits are what real estate investments are all about. While many of the investors prefer buying a property, holding it for years and then selling it when the time is right, many others rent the property to earn additional monthly income. But which is actually better? Capital appreciation or the income from rent?

While the question seems simple, the answer to it isn't. There are several aspects that need to be considered to know whether capital appreciation or income from rent is the better way to earn healthy returns from a particular real estate investment. Especially in India, where there can be a major difference in the real estate costs even within the same neighbourhood, it is very important to create proper balance between capital appreciation and rent to get the best of both worlds.

Answering this important question and some amazing tips for investors looking to let out their property on rent to increase their rental income and use the income to build assets are some of the aspects that are discussed in this section.

CHAPTER 1

TIPS TO BUY A HIGH RENT YIELDING PROPERTY

Buying properties in lakhs and selling it off a few years later in crores is primarily the basic idea behind the concept of real estate investment in India. However, it is important to note that the entire procedure does involve a very long period of time.

Many people take the alternative option and invest in real estate properties to earn rental income while the total cost of property appreciates over a period of time. Rental income is rather a quicker and easier option which comes with an excellent opportunity to earn additional money every month. Investors who are looking to buy a real estate property with a plan to put it on rent, the following tips can be of real help.

1. SELECTION OF AN AREA THAT IS PROMISING

The area in and around the property should have a social value not just in terms of cost but also a desirable appeal in terms of location where people would love to live. This factor may not be an immediate need but definitely an essential one in the days to come. For instance, there are certain locations where proposals of building shopping complex, hospital, banks, metro railways are proposed that will definitely make the property a high-yielding one in the coming days.

2. WRITE THINGS DOWN

As mentioned earlier, buying a real estate property is an investment and all investments must be a result of well-thought out decisions. Pen down your budget to invest, the amount of loan you would be able to manage, and the rent-value of the property. Besides, one should not forget to include the maintenance cost of the property in the check list. This actually is extremely beneficial for the broker or real estate agent who can narrow down the search of properties to the criteria provided by the investor.

3. WHAT KIND OF TENANTS YOU ARE LOOKING FOR?

Finding the right tenant is complimentary to your investment plan and hence choosing the right tenant plays a crucial role. The location of the property also helps in assessing the kind of tenant that your property can fetch. For instance, if the property is close to a college or hostel, the tenants can be students who are looking for a property that is comfortable and easy to clean. Young professionals would look for a property that is stylish and modern but not anything overbearing. And if the tenant tends to shift with family, they will need larger empty spaces for their belongings. Hence, proximity to different institutions is crucial to selection of the tenant.

The above-mentioned tips can help an investor buy a high rent yielding property. But with such properties, it is very important to not be over-ambitious and make sure that the rent is in line with other similar properties in the locality.

Many of the investors believe that letting out the property on rent is a tiring effort and hence they prefer to only take advantage of the appreciation in property rate over time. While it certainly depends on the preferences of an investor, it is important to create a balance between appreciation and rent to get the best returns.

APPRECIATION V/S RENT: FINDING A BALANCE

Gross difference in real estate properties in the same locality is found in India which many investors find quite shocking and unbelievable. There are two aspects to this kind of phenomenon based on investment strategy. There are some who invest high amount of money to buy properties in posh locations and hence would ask for a higher rent. There are others who invest less money to buy properties in mediocre neighbourhoods and wait for these areas to develop to earn handsome appreciation in future.

Unlike the stock market, which are comparatively easier to understand on the basis of the index which determines the market sentiment, the performance of the real estate properties are a lot difficult to comprehend. As a result, investors who prefer to let out their properties on rent and the investors who wait for appreciation are both right from their own perspectives.

So, What is More Important, Appreciation or Rent?

The reality is that both of them are equally important.

> **The expectation from real estate investments is different for different investors. Hence, appreciation and rent both are two crucial yardsticks before planning to go for real estate investment.**

Hence it is crucial to do a fair research on the extent the property rates can appreciate in the area as well as the rental income that you can generate, will allow you to understand the duration for which you should hold on to the property.

APPRECIATION STRATEGY

Investors who buy real estate property on the basis of the appreciation strategy do so due to a number of reasons, like funding for their retirement, supporting their children, or as a hedge against their savings. Such investors should go for properties that are located in central areas, are somewhat luxurious and they themselves can live in the property if required.

As the investment will be done for a very long duration, it is important to invest in areas that carry great future potential. Tier II and Tier III cities in India that are rapidly expanding can be great for such investments.

RENTAL STRATEGY

Investors who let out their property on rent generally do so to earn additional income or actual income if the investor is retired. For such investors, areas that can undergo substantial change in near future can make the real estate property a high-yielding one. They can go for larger as well as smaller properties that are not exactly in central locations but have strong demand from a rental perspective. Properties close to schools, colleges, shopping malls, railway stations, employment hubs help a lot in getting a great rental income.

Appreciation and rental strategy both carry great potential and thus, both of them should be considered equally before making the investment. As an investor, it is very significant to understand what kind of returns you are expecting from the property as this helps you to choose the right property best suited to your needs.

TIPS TO MULTIPLY YOUR RENTAL INCOME

If an investor already has a property which they have let out on rent or investors who are looking to buy a property which they can let out, it is very important to first maximize the profits on your investment before looking for other investment options. The below mentioned tips can help investors multiply their rental income.

1. MINIMIZE VACANCY

It is very important for an investor to keep vacancy to minimum to enjoy better rental income. And the best way to do so is to look for tenants who will live in the property for a long term. Avoid renting out to people who are between jobs or are looking to buy their own house soon. As the vacancy will reduce, the investor will receive rental income on a consistent basis without the need to look for tenants time and again.

2. REDUCE THE TURNOVER

There are many different ways in which turnover costs a significant amount of money. While looking for new tenants, the investor needs to give advertisements in newspapers and websites, do the minor painting and patching work, and mange the vacancy as you will not earn rental income. To reduce the turnover, a lot of investors keep the property rent slightly lesser than the average rent in the area to get better tenants and avoid vacancy.

 **One of the most important goals for every landlord is to look for quality tenants who will take care of the property, live for long term and pay the rent regularly. And when the investor finally finds such tenants, they should do everything possible to keep them happy.**

3. STRATEGICALLY INCREASE THE RENT

It is true that tenants do stick to your property for long when they cannot find a similar property at a lower rent. But this does not mean that the investor should avoid increasing the rent altogether. It is important to remember that moving to a new place involves costs for the tenants too, and if the increase in rent at the current place is lower than the costs that the tenants would spend in moving to a new place, the investor will still have an edge. The important thing here is to do it strategically.

For instance, if an investor is looking to get the home painted or upgrade the windows, they can do so when it's time to renew the lease. This can be an excellent way to increase the rent in the new lease as the tenants would believe that they are getting something in return.

These are some of the tips which investors can use for their properties to gradually increase the rent and earn higher returns on the investment.

HOW TO MAKE YOUR PROPERTY MORE VALUABLE FOR A HIGHER RENT?

After your initial investment in buying the property and then putting it on rent, one of the important assessments includes ensuring that valuation of the property is on an increase. The following are some of the tips that can help you to increase the value of your property with time.

MAKE SURE THAT THE PROPERTY IS CLEAN

If an investor has purchased a resale property, it is very important to make sure that the property is professionally cleaned before showing it to potential tenants. Investors can either choose to do it themselves to give a more personal touch or can hire professionals instead. Cleanliness and neatness are the two aspects which a potential tenant will encounter first when they come for the first visit.

TRY SHOWING THE PROPERTY TO MULTIPLE PARTIES AT A TIME

When showing the property, avoid setting different appointments for the tenants to show the property. Try receiving calls from potential tenants for about 8-10 days and then ask every interested party to show up at the same day and time. The exposure of the property at the same time among multiple potential tenants, will exhibit a demand for the property, which actually works for the advantage of the property owner. This may sometimes allow investors to let out the property to the highest bidder.

TOUCH UP THE ENTRANCE

The first impression towards a property for many gives a lasting effect and every property owner looking for a tenant would love to offer such an impression. So spending some money on the entrance of the home, like painting the door or having an interesting curio outside the door can be really impressive. When potential tenants walk up to the property, they should be able to feel that they can actually live there and they should not take much time to make the judgement. So, ensure that the entrance offers a refreshing look and a warm welcome.

MAKE THE APPLIANCES LOOK GOOD

If an investor already has some essential appliances available in the house, it is very important to ensure that they look as good as new. The perfect condition of these appliances can add up to the impression and may actually help you to get a great deal. It is not necessary that the appliances have to be new ones, but even if it is the used ones, ensuring a neat look and complete usability is important.

The above-mentioned tips are pretty simple to apply, highly effective, and would not involve much monetary expenses.

 **It is also very important for an investor to ensure that the rent of his property is in line with the rent of similar properties in the area.**

Moreover, there are many who are inclined to make expensive modifications or makeovers to the property. This, in fact, is a great idea only if you know that this value addition is going to fetch you higher returns in terms of higher rent.

USING YOUR RENT TO BUILD ASSETS

Apparently, making investments in a real estate property and letting it out on rent to generate additional income, seems like a great idea. The usual trend is to look for a suitable area, buy a property, get a tenant and the money will start rolling in. Increasing number of investors are now looking for buy-to-let properties due to some assured success stories in regard to such investments. However, building assets from rental income is something that is easier said than done.

Real estate property involves a huge amount of monetary investment. Hence, it is very important to be very careful about the whole buy-to-let process and using the income to build assets, especially, for those investors who are doing it for the first time.

The below-mentioned tips can be really helpful.

GIVE A PROFESSIONAL BUSINESS TREATMENT

Investment in multiple buy-to-let properties to generate monthly income may not be a successful scheme for all investors. Real estate investments are a huge commitment and while there is a possibility that an investor can make good money from it, it is very important to treat the whole process like a professional business deal. Your personal involvement in terms of personal research, influential contacts, professional help- a requisite for successful business initiatives, all plays an important role in allowing an investor to successfully handle his buy-to-let portfolio.

LOCAL RESEARCH IS IMPORTANT

To build assets from rental income, finding right property in the right locality is crucial. As an investor, one needs to do a fair amount of research on the kind of property in respect to the locality and also keep in mind the target tenants. If the property is close to parks and school, families will generally be the target audience. Properties close to universities would attract students more than anyone else.

Even the facilities provided in a property should meet the basic demands of the tenants, whatever type they may be. For instance, university students will generally look for properties that are easy to clean and comfortable. By providing these facilities, an investor shouldn't find it difficult to keep the vacancy rates at minimum.

AVOID INVESTING IN RUN-DOWN PROPERTIES

A lot of investors consider buying run-down properties which require major repair work at a lower rate and believe it to be a profitable deal. Unless the property rate is very cheap, such properties generally prove expensive in the longer run. Besides demanding a huge repair work, the property would not be up for rent for a considerable amount of time, hence involving a loss of both money and time which may not be a great investment decision. In case one buys multiple run-down properties, generating the initial amount of investment from the rental income will also take some considerable amount of time.

KNOWING THE RIGHT PEOPLE

If an investor is looking to expand their buy-to-let property portfolio beyond a couple of locations, managing the properties all together can become a difficult task. The investor will need trustworthy contractors that offer high-quality work. Moreover, a great rapport with such contractors makes it easier to negotiate discounts and increase overall profit from the real estate investment. Forming such relationships with professionals take time and if an investor already has such advantages, they will be in a better position.

While some mistakes in this entire process are inevitable, the investor needs to ensure that such mistakes are handled well at the right time. These mistakes sometimes become learning experiences and will take an investor closer to a profitable portfolio of multiple buy-to-let properties.

CHAPTER 2

BUILDING WEALTH FROM YOUR INVESTMENT

The world of real estate investments has its own complications and confusions, which is also the reason why only a few investors are able to consistently make profits. Right from choosing between earning money from capital appreciation or from rent, to understanding the relation between inflation and appreciation, a successful investor is required to know a number of things to make right choices.

Apart from the traditional ways of earning returns from real estate investment i.e. by capital appreciation and rent, there are modern terms as well like flipping of properties, REIT, etc. that make the whole real estate investment process too complicated for new investors. While these things might look too confusing initially, they are not that difficult to understand and any investor with only a basic amount of knowledge in the real estate sector can understand them.

Some of these age-old questions and the modern alternatives to traditional approaches are discussed in this section.

INFLATION AND APPRECIATION: KNOW YOUR STANDING

There is a major relation between inflation and appreciation of the real estate prices. As a matter of fact, inflation has a correlation with every single good that is only available in limited quantity. For instance, let us consider an economy which is made up of Rs. 100 and has 10 houses in the entire economy without any other kind of goods in the economy. As a result, the cost of every house in this economy would be Rs. 10 each. Now, if the RBI provides more money and the total money in the economy becomes Rs. 200, every house would now be priced at Rs. 20.

It is very easy to see in this simple example that increase in money supply leads to inflation, which ultimately increases the cost of real estate properties. While this example demonstrates a direct link between inflation and appreciation, there are many other ways in which inflation affects the appreciation of real estate prices.

LEVERAGE

Real estate properties are considered as great assets from the perspective of inflation. This is because property rates will rise with inflation and the asset is leveraged. While purchasing a property, you are required to make a down-payment of at least 20%-30% of the total cost of the property. The cost of the property will rise by multiplying the cost of the property with the rise in inflation and not by multiplying the down-payment amount with inflation.

 **So, if the inflation is doubled, cost of the property might have quadrupled the down-payment amount. In such a scenario, fixed-rate home loan can be a better option as the investor will be required to pay the amount which is congruent to the inflation and as a result, the investor will be required to repay lesser amount as compared to what had been calculated before.**

MODERATING FACTORS

Just like other goods, the prices of real estate properties are also influenced by this system of supply and demand. Even if there is an oversupply of real estate properties when inflation is high, their cost will not rise along with inflation. This is because when the inflation rates go up, the interest rates tend to get higher as well. And when the interest rates are higher, people will avoid real estate investment, leading to a decline in demand of real estate properties. As a result, the prices will tend to remain static, and if the supply continues, the prices will start going down.

While inflation in India is pretty much under control since the last few years, appreciation of property rates due to rising inflation reflects an unlikely scenario. With inflation out of the picture, it is only the demand and supply that can further increase the cost of properties in India.

REIT IN INDIA:
A FAD OR A RISING TREND

Real Estate Investment Trusts or REITs are promoted as an excellent alternative to buying a real estate property directly. Investment in an REIT is similar to investment in stocks which can be traded publicly in the market. These trusts make use of the collected capital of the investors to purchase mortgage loans, known as Mortgage REIT and/or income property, known as Equity REIT.

> Apart from the normal investors, there are also Trustees, Managers, Sponsors and the Principal Valuer who are part of REITs. People who do not have enough money to invest in a real estate property but still want to earn income from the real estate sector generally invest in REITs. Moreover, they are also an excellent investment alternative for investors who are looking to diversify their portfolio.

But just like every other investment option, REITs also come with their share of advantages and disadvantages.

ADVANTAGES OF INVESTING IN REITS

- Higher Dividend- REITs are required to pay 90% of the income they generate to the investors in the form of dividends.

- Diversifying Portfolio- Stock prices are not correlated to the prices of actual real estate properties. While they can rise together, they can move in opposite directions as well. Thus, adding REITs is an excellent way to diversify the investment portfolio.
- Long Leases- Many of the REITs in India have their own real estate properties which they have let out on long term leases. As a result, an investor gets to earn steady and secure income throughout the period of the lease.
- Professional Management- Majority of the REITs are managed by skilled and experienced professionals. Average investors do not generally have the skills required to manage properties that bear higher income.

DISADVANTAGES OF INVESTING IN REITS

- Slower Growth- As 90% of the income is distributed among the investors; REITs only get to reinvest 10% of the income in the important business lines. As a result, most of the REITs grow at a slower rate.
- Cyclical Business Pattern- The income stream of REITs is not guaranteed. The real estate sector is full of cyclical downturns that can make REITs highly unstable.
- Taxes- While REITs are not required to pay taxes on their profits; investors are required to pay tax on the dividends not in the form of capital gains but as their personal income. As a result, the investors who are in high tax brackets might have to pay higher taxes on their income from REITs.

REITs come with their fair share of some solid advantages and disadvantages. While they can be good for investors who want to diversify their portfolio, investors who are just starting to invest in real estate should avoid involvement in investment through REITs.

HOW TO MAKE MONEY BY FLIPPING PROPERTIES?

The usual ways of real estate investment are mainly selling a real estate property at higher rate sooner or later or renting out the property to earn monthly rent. Another way to generate profit is by flipping properties.

WHAT IS PROPERTY FLIPPING?

In short, property flipping is buying a property at a lower rate and then reselling the same within few months for a profit. Now the question remains, how profitable is this venture. In countries other than India, there are full-time property flippers who have actually made a substantial amount of money. However, it is important to know that bad decisions can make an investor end up losing everything in the process. But when done carefully, things can actually work out.

HOW TO FLIP A PROPERTY?

1. EDUCATE YOURSELF

Buying a cheap house and then selling it for a profit is not as easy as it sounds. It is very important to educate yourself about the entire process of flipping properties to actually strike a profitable deal. For starters, the initial knowledge comes from studying the local real estate market and the kind of properties in current demand. Remember that the future prospects of a particular area should not be taken into consideration as the property will be sold within a few months.

2. LOOK FOR AN EXPERIENCED FLIPPER

If an investor already knows someone who has experience with flipping, their guidance can be of great help. An investor can also consider offering them a small incentive from the profits, as part of the consultation or guidance fee. This is an excellent way to keep a flipping mentor motivated and make sure that they provide all the important information. Also, if an investor is open to offering financial incentives or consultation fees, then a good number of experts would be interested to work for the investor despite not having a personal rapport.

3. INITIAL OFFER

The initial offer that an investor makes for a property ascertains the amount of money the investor can gain from the property later. If a particular property is being sold at a lower rate, an investor will surely have some competition. So, before making the offer, an investor should know the maximum amount he can pay for the property. This maximum price will be an amount that the investor can pay to the current owner and still easily make profits.

The money to be spent on the property for repairs, taxes and interest should also be considered. In case the deal does not provide a profitable outlook, there is always a personal discretion to walk away from the investment and look for another property. Every investor should never forget the fact that profit should be the sole yardstick behind every deal.

There is no denying the fact that property flipping comes with a fair share of rewards and risks. If an investor can handle all these ups and downs, flipping property can be an excellent choice for them. And if there be a little bit of doubt and fear regarding such kind of real estate investment, then the standard methods of appreciation or letting out the property on rent should be obtained.

LAND VS. FLATS? WHICH APPRECIATES BETTER? (LONG TERM AND SHORT TERM)

While investing in real estate, one of the most common confusions rises from choosing whether to invest in a piece of land or in an apartment. The reality is that both kinds of investments come with their own share of advantages and drawbacks. Thus, it is very important for the investor to understand his requirements to make a smart investing decision.

While investing in land provides an investor with the ability to build a house as per their own requirement, flats come with better accessibility and security. Some of the most important factors that an investor should thoroughly evaluate in this respect are mentioned below -

APPRECIATION

Real estate investments are all about appreciation. So, when it comes to choosing between land and apartments on the basis of appreciation, it is the land that provides better returns. This is because land is a resource that is limited and thus, it appreciates faster as compared to apartments or flats of same dimension in a similar location and within the same time-frame.

POSSESSION

While purchasing land, the possession is immediate if the land is not part of any developer's project. On the other hand, possession of a flat is only given when the entire project is completed. There are several instances where projects get delayed and as a result, the possession of a flat can be consequently delayed as well.

RISK AND CONSTRUCTION QUALITY

 If a plot of land is not fenced or if the fencing is not strong enough, encroachment is an imminent threat.

Apartments, from this perspective, are secure and safe from encroachment problems. If the construction quality is considered, when a house is being constructed on a plot of land, the owner can closely monitor the entire construction process to ensure that the construction is of high quality. However, with flats and apartments, it is the builder who is responsible for the quality of construction and many of them often compromise the quality to meet deadlines and reduce construction costs.

FINANCE AND TAX

Investors are required to have a sound financial condition to invest in a plot of land. While there are banks and other financial institutions that offer loans to purchase land, it becomes a long-term process. Moreover, the tax benefits that are associated with buying a piece of land are available for the first year of purchase and are subject to completion of the construction project on the land. Buying flats on the other hand is a simpler process. Home loans are widely available at competitive interest rates and the buyer can avail a number of tax benefits as well.

INCOME

The only way to generate income from a piece of land is by selling it. But flats and apartments can be let out on rent to earn consistent additional income on a monthly basis. And with the tenancy laws now in place, the litigation scope is very limited.

Real estate investment is undoubtedly one of the best forms of investment. However, when it comes to selecting between buying a piece of land or a flat, an investor should consider both the advantages and disadvantages from their own standpoint to make a sound decision.

WHY SHOULD YOU NOT LIVE IN THE HOUSE YOU BUY?

People who are young and are looking to buy a new home for themselves are often advised to turn their first purchase into investment property. People generally buy a home or two before they start thinking about investing in real estate properties. However, it is true that buyers can start investing in real estate properties much sooner.

While the idea of turning the first home into an investment property clearly goes against the age-old personal finance notions, it is very important to change the beliefs with time. The general approach to post-college life in India is-

- To get a job
- First move to a rental house
- Marriage
- Then buy a house
- Plan to have a child
- Buy a second house
- Education of the child
- Investments

Though this approach has been successful for generations, with changing times, evolving out of this stereotyped notion of investment can be beneficial in the long run. With the above-mentioned approach, an individual will easily be in their late 30s or early 40s before they even start thinking about investments. This will not provide them with enough time to let their investments grow and provide them with substantial returns.

There are many different benefits of not living in the house you buy. Some of them are -

AGE BENEFIT

Being independent and young is definitely an amazing feeling. However, this feeling gets diluted quickly when you are bound to consider your other goals in life. The life that people in their early 20s live provides them with a number of opportunities to cut costs and accumulate enough money for making down-payment of a home and then renting it out to pay the EMI. This cost-cutting might not be an option at a later stage in life where there will be an increased amount of responsibilities.

ADDITIONAL SOURCE OF INCOME

Even if you have a great salary, an extra income will actually add up. By purchasing a property and letting it out on rent, an individual can quickly start earning additional monthly income. This money can then be used for making other investments, paying EMIs, or paying other debts and bills.

CHANGING DEMOGRAPHICS

Increasing number of people in India are now looking to be homeowners. As the demand grows with time, property rates would increase too and an investment in a good property now can actually turn up to be an extremely profitable investment in a decade. Even financial experts insist on real estate investments at an early age.

While purchasing a home is undoubtedly one of the biggest achievements of life, the current dynamics require an individual to do something different to get better financial results as compared to others. Letting out the first property on rent or selling it after capital appreciation, is undoubtedly a great way to stay ahead of others and keep the financial future secure.

DOCUMENTS TO HAVE AS A BUYER

Every buyer should have the below mentioned documents-

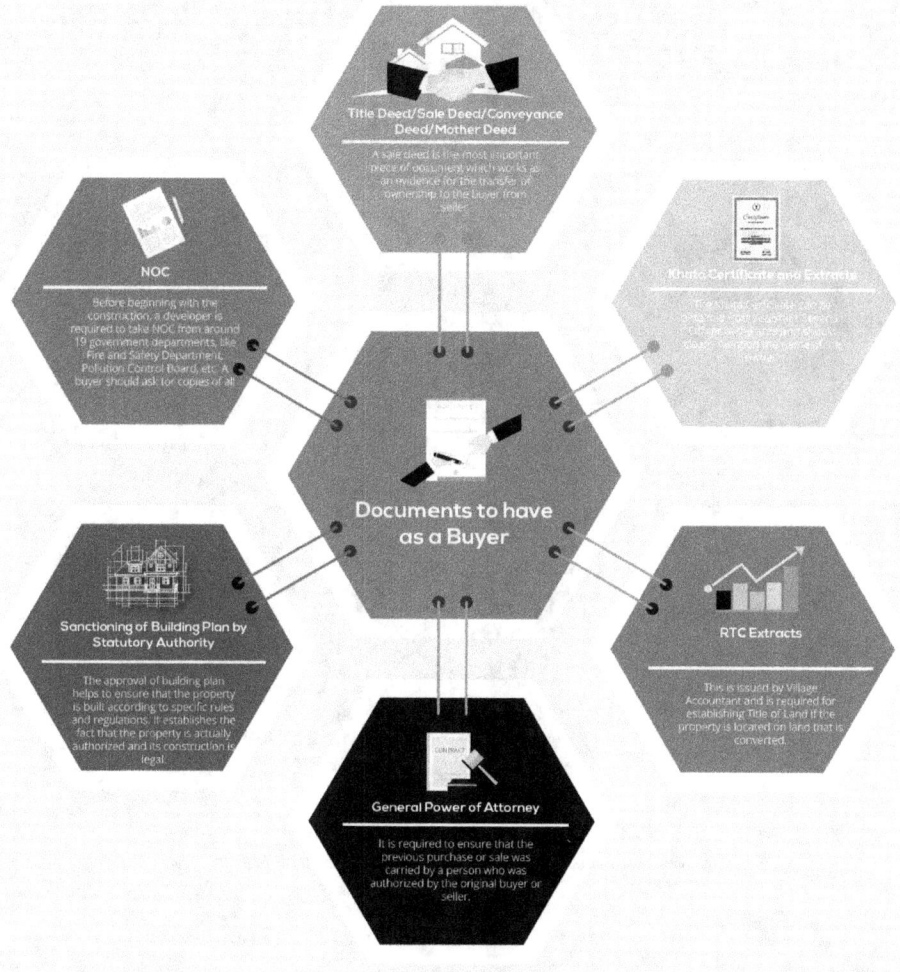

Title Deed/Sale Deed/Conveyance Deed/Mother Deed

A sale deed is the most important piece of document which works as an evidence for the transfer of ownership to the buyer from seller.

NOC

Before beginning with the construction, a developer is required to take NOC from around 19 government departments, like Fire and Safety Department, Pollution Control Board, etc. A buyer should ask for copies of all.

Khata Certificate and Extracts

The Khata certificate can be among the most important documents of property transaction, which identifies the owner of the estate.

Documents to have as a Buyer

Sanctioning of Building Plan by Statutory Authority

The approval of building plan helps to ensure that the property is built according to specific rules and regulations. It establishes the fact that the property is actually authorized and its construction is legal.

RTC Extracts

This is issued by Village Accountant and is required for establishing Title of Land if the property is located on land that is converted.

General Power of Attorney

It is required to ensure that the previous purchase or sale was carried by a person who was authorized by the original buyer or seller.

Inspection of Property before Signing a Deal

Some of the most important things that a buyer should definitely check during an inspection includes-

Walls that back bathrooms

While inspecting the house, make sure that the walls that back the bathrooms are thoroughly inspected for signs of water leaks or moisture penetration.

Ceilings

Look at all the ceilings to make sure that they are fixed firmly in place and are not sagging or have a parachute-like appearance.

Mould in Bedroom or Bathroom

A buyer will be required to hire a professional remediation company to remove the mould and this can be an expensive affair.

Cracks on Walls

External as well as internal wall should be visually checked for large cracks.

Wall Plastering

The plastering on the internal wall can be inspected for hairline cracks which are also known as map cracks because they look similar to a map.

HOW TO CHECK THE DOCUMENTS OF A PROPERTY

To make sure that the real estate transaction is free from litigations, there are a few factors that an investor can keep in mind.

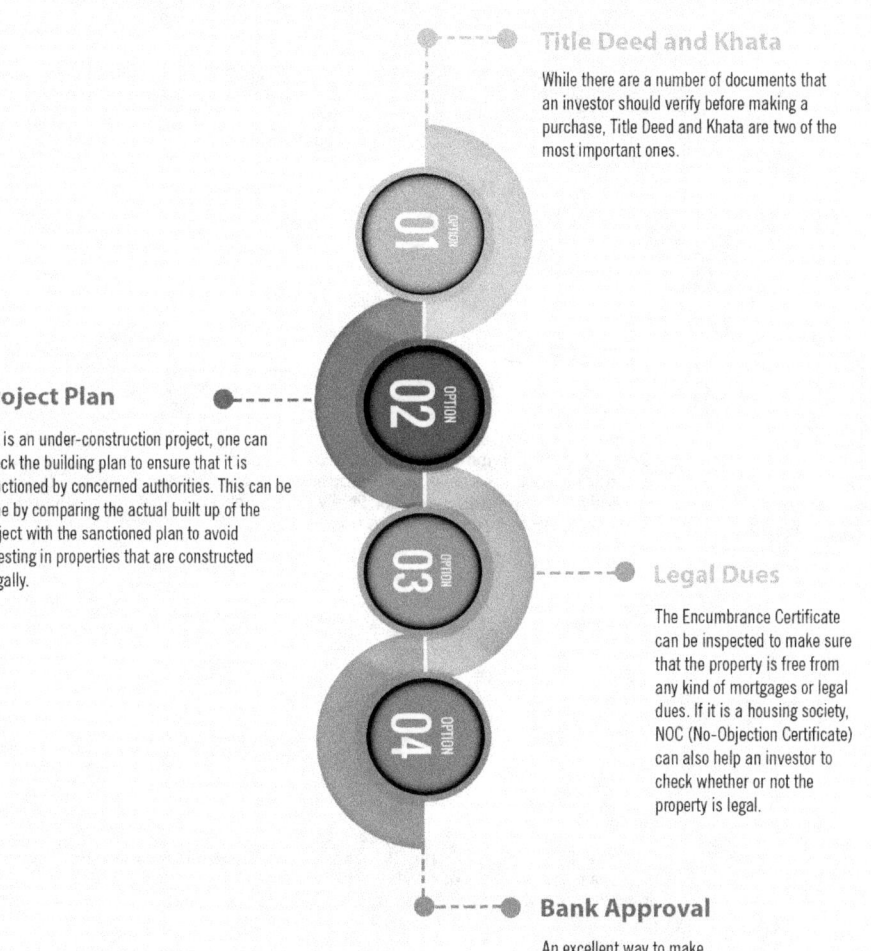

Title Deed and Khata

While there are a number of documents that an investor should verify before making a purchase, Title Deed and Khata are two of the most important ones.

Project Plan

If it is an under-construction project, one can check the building plan to ensure that it is sanctioned by concerned authorities. This can be done by comparing the actual built up of the project with the sanctioned plan to avoid investing in properties that are constructed illegally.

Legal Dues

The Encumbrance Certificate can be inspected to make sure that the property is free from any kind of mortgages or legal dues. If it is a housing society, NOC (No-Objection Certificate) can also help an investor to check whether or not the property is legal.

Bank Approval

An excellent way to make sure whether or not a property is legal is a bank approval.

Tips to Multiply Your Rental Income

The below mentioned tips can help investors multiply their rental income.

1

MINIMIZE VACANCY

It is very important for an investor to keep vacancy to minimum to enjoy better rental income. And the best way to do is to look for tenants who will live in the property for a long-term

2

REDUCE THE TURNOVER

One of the most important goals for every landlord is to look for quality tenants who will take care of the property, live for long-term and pay the rent regularly. And when the investor finally finds such tenants, they should do everything possible to keep them happy.

3

STRATEGICALLY INCREASE THE RENT

It is true that the tenants do stick to your property for long when they cannot find a similar property at a lower rent. But this does not mean that the investor should avoid increasing the rent altogether.

How to make your Property more Valuable for a Higher Rent

The following are some of the tips that can help you to increase the value of your property with time.

Make sure that the Property is Clean

Try Showing the Property to Multiple Parties at a Time

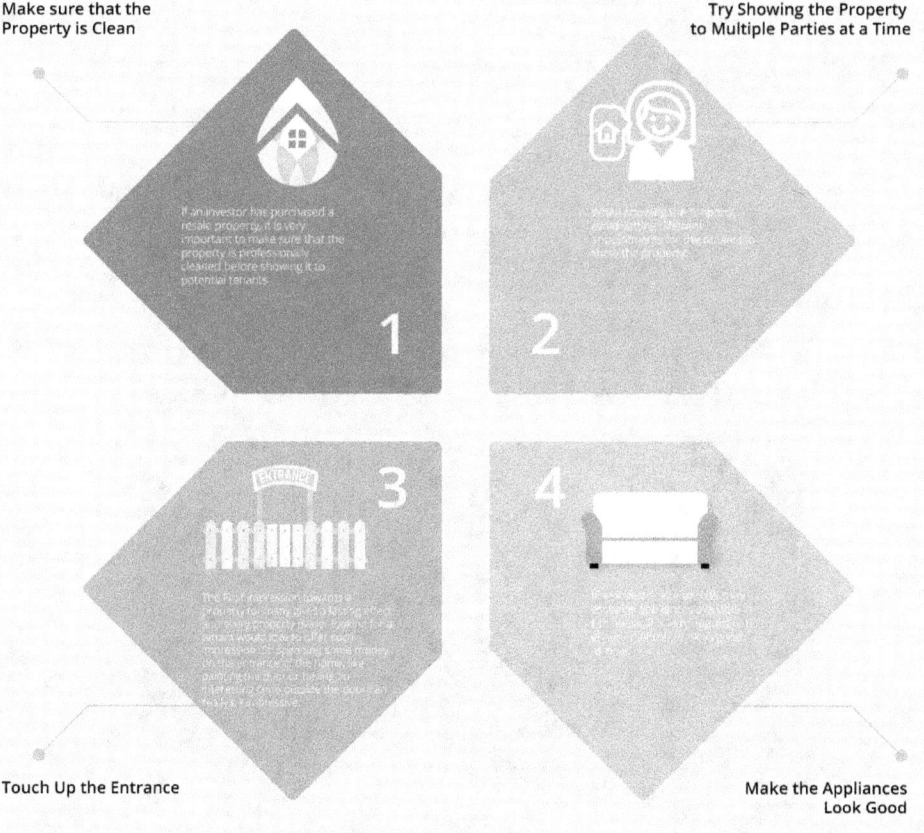

Touch Up the Entrance

Make the Appliances Look Good

REIT IN INDIA: A FAD OR A RISING TREND

(Just like every other investment option,
REITs also come with their share of advantages and disadvantages)

ADVANTAGES OF INVESTING IN REITS

01

HIGHER DIVIDEND

REITs are required to pay 90% of the income they generate to the investors in the form of dividends

02

DIVERSIFYING PORTFOLIO

Stock prices are not correlated to the prices of actual real estate properties. While they can rise together, they can move in opposite directions as well

03

LONG LEASES

Many of the REITs in India have their own real estate properties which they have let out on long term leases

04

PROFESSIONAL MANAGEMENT

Majority of the REITs is managed by skilled and experienced professionals

DISADVANTAGES OF INVESTING IN REITS

01

SLOWER GROWTH

As 90% of the income is distributed among the investors, REITs only get to reinvest 10% of the income in the important business lines. As a result, most of the REITs grow at a slower rate

02

CYCLICAL BUSINESS PATTERN

The income stream of REITs is not guaranteed. The real estate sector is full of cyclical downturns that can make REITs highly unstable

03

TAXES

While REITs are not required to pay taxes on their profits, investors are required to pay tax on the dividends not in the form of capital gains but as their personal income

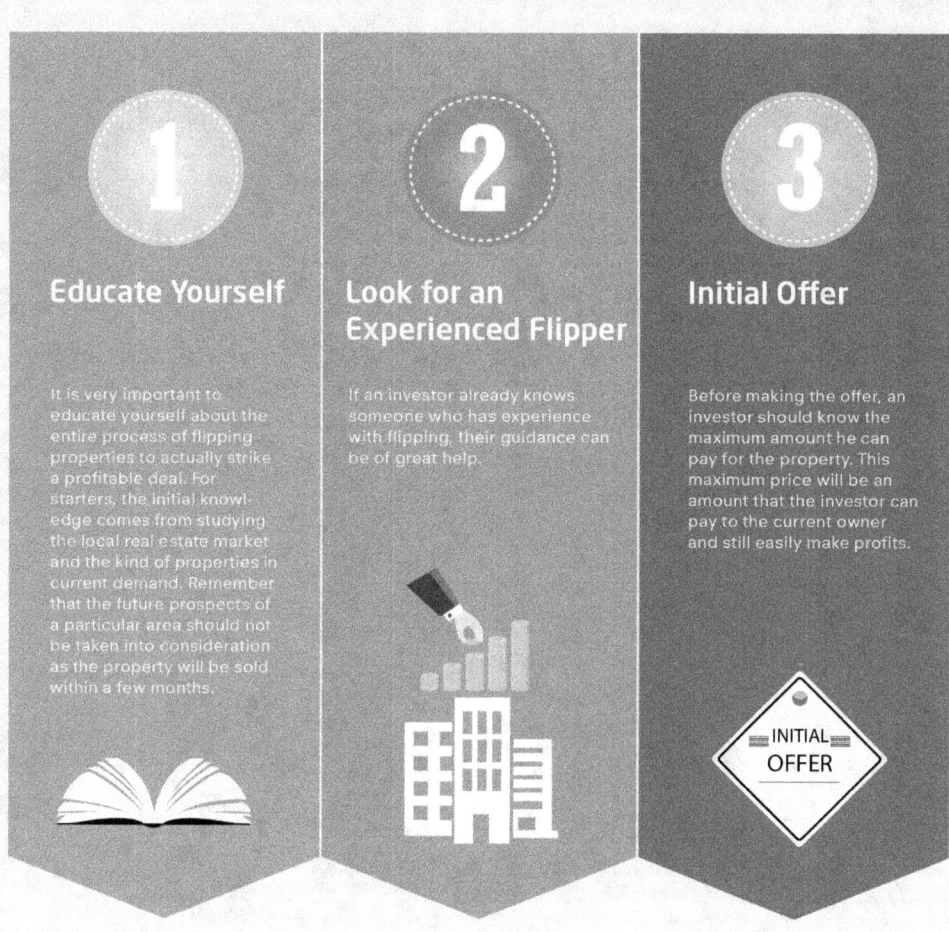

1
Educate Yourself

It is very important to educate yourself about the entire process of flipping properties to actually strike a profitable deal. For starters, the initial knowledge comes from studying the local real estate market and the kind of properties in current demand. Remember that the future prospects of a particular area should not be taken into consideration as the property will be sold within a few months.

2
Look for an Experienced Flipper

If an investor already knows someone who has experience with flipping, their guidance can be of great help.

3
Initial Offer

Before making the offer, an investor should know the maximum amount he can pay for the property. This maximum price will be an amount that the investor can pay to the current owner and still easily make profits.

INITIAL OFFER

How to Make Money by Flipping Properties

LAND VS. FLATS?
WHICH APPRECIATES BETTER?
(LONG TERM AND SHORT TERM)

Some of the most important factors that an investor should thoroughly evaluate in this respect are mentioned below-

05 Income

The only way to generate income from a piece of land is by selling it. But flats and apartments can be let out on rent to earn consistent additional income on a monthly basis.

01 Appreciation

Real estate investments are all about appreciation. So, when it comes to choosing between land and apartments on the basis of appreciation, it is the land that provides better returns.

04 Finance and Tax

Investors are required to have a sound financial condition to invest in a plot of land. While there are banks and other financial institutions that offer loans to purchase land, it becomes a long term process.. Buying flats on the other hand is a simpler process.

02 Possession

While purchasing land, the possession is immediate if the land is not part of any developer's project. On the other hand, possession of a flat is only given when the entire project is completed.

03 Risk and Construction Quality

If a plot of land is not fenced or if the fencing is not strong enough, encroachment is an imminent threat. Apartments, from this perspective, are secure and safe from encroachment problems.

CHAPTER 3

DON'T LET THE TAXMAN EAT INTO YOUR WEALTH

The real estate market, deep down, is a field of investment that involves a number of hidden expenditures and costs. And when the taxes are added to this minefield, it can actually drive an investor to tears. Irrespective of whether an investor is buying or selling a real estate property, taxman keeps an eye on every single real estate transaction. So, there are no legal ways to actually run away from taxes.

While an investor cannot completely avoid paying taxes in real estate transactions, professional advice can reduce it to highly palatable levels. Be it an Indian resident or NRI, buying or selling a real estate property in India or an Indian resident investing in real estate properties abroad, there are many useful ways in which the tax burden can be reduced.

Over the years, there have been a number of changes to the Income Tax Laws to make things easier for the buyers and the same are discussed in this section.

TIPS TO SAVE TAXES ON RENTAL INCOME

Income from the rent of a property in India is deemed as an income that is accumulated from India and is taxable under the Income Tax Act, irrespective of your residential status. But if the taxable income from India, along with the rental income, is not higher than the limit of non-taxable income (Rs. 2.5 lakhs), you may not have to pay taxes on your rental income.

Moreover, the total amount of rent that you receive is not completely taxable as there are many deductions, like -

- Standard deductions (30%)
- Interest which is paid on loan that is taken for renewal, repair, construction, or acquisition of property
- Municipal taxes
- Interest deduction during the pre-construction phase

Apart from these, if the property is purchased with a bank loan, even the repayment of the principal amount is eligible for tax deductions under section 80C.

If the rental income is higher than the maximum limit of non-taxable income, there are several ways to save taxes.

1. DECLARE THE HIGHER RENTAL VALUE PROPERTY AS SELF-OCCUPIED

If you have more than one property, you can declare the property with higher rental value as self-occupied, irrespective of whether or not you actually live in that property. This will allow you to only pay taxes on the rental income of the property with lower rental value.

2. PAY PROPERTY TAX OR MUNICIPAL TAX ON TIME

You can also get reductions on property or municipal taxes for the rental income. However, you should pay these taxes in the current financial year. As there is no way to escape from the Government taxes, paying it on time and then claiming it as tax reduction can allow you to save money.

3. GO FOR A JOINT PROPERTY

Buying a joint property along with your spouse is often a great investment strategy. The rental income will then be divided in two as there will be two owners of the same property. As a result, the contribution of rental income in determining your maximum non-taxable income will get automatically reduced.

4. ASK TENANT TO PAY FOR ADDITIONAL FACILITIES

Many of the owners provide additional facilities, like gas connection, Wi-Fi, cable/DTH TV, etc. to their tenants. The charges for such facilities are generally included in the rent which the owner then pays to the concerned authorities. However, a better option is to ask the tenant to pay for these services themselves and you can then reduce this amount from the rent to save tax on rental income.

It is important for an owner to understand the components of rental income tax and how it is computed to reduce the amount of tax the owner pays for receiving such a rent. While the tax cannot be completely avoided, better planning can help in reducing it.

Just like rental income tax, certain smart decisions can help you reduce the amount of tax you pay for selling a property.

AVOIDING BIG TAX BILLS ON YOUR PROPERTY SALE

Profit generated from selling of a capital asset, like property, is known as Capital Gains. These gains are subject to capital gains tax of the Income Tax Act.

If a property has been owned by you for a period of less than three years and you sell this property, you will be required to pay short term capital gains tax and if you owned the property for more than three years before selling it, you need to pay long term capital gains tax. Short term capital gains tax is based on the income tax slab under which the owner pays income tax, whereas, long term capital gains tax is fixed at 20% and can run in to several lakhs.

Needless to say, no one really wants to pay such huge tax amounts. Fortunately, there are several ways to reduce the capital gains tax and protect yourself from the tax burden.

1. INVEST THE GAINS IN RESIDENTIAL PROPERTY (SECTION 54/54F)

Under Section 54/54F of the IT Act, the long term capital gains that arise from the sale of capital assets are exempted if the net sale amount is again invested in construction or purchase of a single residential property.

However, the new property should be purchased at least one year before the sale of the current property or within two years from the date on which the current property is sold. If the gains are used for constructing a new residential property, it should be done within three years from the date on which the current property is sold.

2. CAPITAL GAINS ACCOUNT SCHEME

If the new property is not constructed or acquired before the last date of filing of returns for the current year, the amount that will be invested in the property can be deposited in a CGA (Capital Gains Account) of authorized banks. But if the amount that is deposited in the CGA remains unused until three years from the date of sale of the previous property, it will be taxable in that same year.

3. INVEST IN BONDS

If you don't want to immediately invest in a new property after selling your existing property, you can deposit the gains in bonds that are issued by NHAI (National Highway Authority of India) or REC (Rural Electrification Corporation) within six months from the date of sale and it will be exempted under Section 54 EC. You are allowed to invest up to Rs. 50 lakhs in a financial year in these bonds.

However, you will not be allowed to sell the bonds up to three years from the date at which the property was sold. Make sure that you invest in the bonds before the due date of filing returns, so that you can successfully claim exemption. Currently, you get an interest rate of 6% on these investments on bonds. However, the income from the interest will be taxable.

 **Capital gains are not treated like regular income when it comes to computing the taxes. Thus, it is very important to know all the available options to save on your tax liability.**

TIPS TO SAVE TAXES WHILE BUYING PROPERTY

While lot of people buy multiple homes, for many Indians buying a single house in a lifetime is counted as one of the biggest achievements of their life. The Government of India is well-acquainted with this mind-set and hence allows tax deductions when the property is purchased on loan. A borrower is allowed to claim deductions of up to Rs. 1.5 lakhs under Section 80C of the IT Act and if it is a self-occupied property, deductions up to Rs. 2 lakhs are allowed under Section 24 (b).

If a potential buyer takes loan from a company or employer to buy the property, the loan is eligible for deductions. However, the borrower needs to have a proof of records which states that the interest is payable from the company. If a buyer is purchasing an under-construction property, the construction should be completed within three years of application of tax deduction.

There are a few ways through which a property buyer can save paying taxes.

BOOKING UNDER-CONSTRUCTION PROPERTY

Booking an under-construction property can be an economical move from the perspective of saving on taxes. The interest which is paid in the construction period is eligible for tax deductions when paid in five equivalent instalments between the date when the construction began and the date of the possession of the apartment. This way, the buyer can save up to Rs. 2 lakh on taxes in a year. However, it is important that the possession or construction of the property is completed in three years from the date on which the loan was sanctioned. If it exceeds the three years' time frame, tax deduction of only Rs. 30,000 will be allowed.

HRA ALLOWANCE

People who have more than one property can also claim HRA allowance along with the loan deductions under certain conditions. Lot of people do claim HRA by showing receipts of rent they pay to their spouse or parents if the property is on their name. HRA can be claimed when the properties are in different cities as well as in the same city if the reasons are deemed as genuine. For instance, many people in Mumbai and Delhi own a property in far-off suburbs, making it difficult for them to commute to their workplace on a daily basis. This allows the person to claim home loan deductions as well as HRA.

JOINT-PURCHASE

Buyers can also jointly purchase the house with their spouse. In this case, both the husband and wife will get tax deductions of up to Rs. 2 lakhs. Moreover, if the owner's daughter or son is working, the loan can also be split between the owner, spouse and with siblings. As a result, all the three partners will be eligible for loan deductions of up to Rs. 2 lakhs.

While these tax implications and tax-saving tips are applicable to all Indians, things are a little different when an NRI wants to buy or sell a property in India.

TAX IMPLICATIONS FOR NRIs WHILE SELLING AND BUYING PROPERTY IN INDIA

With the value of rupee dropping constantly, real estate has become a lucrative market for NRIs looking to buy and sell properties in India. Most of the NRIs come from Singapore, US, UK, Canada, South Africa, and Middle East. Although buying and selling is effortless, NRIs should know the different tax implications while selling and buying properties in India.

TAX IMPLICATIONS FOR NRIs WHILE SELLING A PROPERTY IN INDIA

TAXATION

NRIs selling their purchased property after three years from the date of purchase will incur a capital gain tax of 20 percent whether the property is inherited or purchased.

If the NRI is selling the property before three years have elapsed from the date of purchase, the NRI will incur a short term capital gain and is subjected to a TDS based on the tax slabs applicable in India.

Furthermore, the resident country of the NRI also plays a crucial role as India has signed DTAA (Double Taxation Avoidance Agreement) with 88 countries for the benefits of NRIs. Therefore, the tax deduction will depend upon whether the resident country has a DTAA enforced with India.

TAX EXEMPTIONS

Under different tax sections, NRIs are eligible for tax exemptions.

Section 54 – According to this section, if the NRI sells the property after three years from purchase date, and reinvests the money in another residential property within two years from the date of sale, the profit generated is exempt to the cost of the new property. However, NRIs cannot reinvest in a property outside India and still avail the benefits of Section 54.

Section 54EC - According to this section, the NRI sells the property after three years from the purchase date, and invests the money in bonds of REC and NHAI within six months from the purchase date, the NRI is exempt from paying taxes. However, bonds will remain locked for a period of three years.

Section 54F – According to this section, if the NRI selling any capital asset other than residential property is eligible for exemption, if they purchase one house property within one year from the transfer date or two years after the transfer date or build one new house property within three years after the transfer of the capital asset. The new house property should mandatorily be located in India and cannot be sold within three years from the purchase date.

However, if the NRI sells the new house or bonds within three years of buying, the tax exemption granted is withdrawn and appropriate tax is levied.

TAX IMPLICATIONS FOR NRIs WHILE BUYING A PROPERTY IN INDIA

As per FEMA, an NRI can purchase an immovable property in India other than plantation, agricultural or farm house. When purchasing a property from the resident Indian, the NRI has to pay tax at one percent if the total value of the house exceeds Rs. 50 lakhs. This taxation is applicable to the first property alone, for subsequent properties, tax is deducted at a rate of one percent the value in excess of Rs. 30 lakhs. Furthermore, the NRI is exempted from wealth tax if the property is vacant and is declared as 'self-occupied'. If the NRI wants to waive the wealth tax, they have to rent the property for 300 days a year.

TAX IMPLICATIONS FOR INDIANS WHILE BUYING OR SELLING PROPERTY ABROAD

Apart from India, many Indians also invest in properties in foreign countries. Just like India, taxes are applied on these transactions as well. However, before buying a property in a foreign country, it is very important to closely look at the economical and political risk in investment in countries other than India. Before investing in a property abroad, the buyer should clearly understand every aspect of buying, along with the direct and indirect costs associated with the purchase.

TAX IMPLICATIONS FOR INDIANS WHILE BUYING PROPERTY ABROAD

Indian residents are allowed to take $250,000 of their funds out of India every year. However, this limit can be increased by going for a joint-property. This will allow your partner to also take $250,000 out of India every year. Investors looking for loans from Indian financial institutions can only take loan in Indian currency for these transactions after taking permission from the Reserve Bank of India (RBI).

> If the loan is taken from a bank outside India, the interest that is paid on the loan is tax-deductible. However, the principal amount is not deductible unless the loan is not taken from particular Indian financial institutions.

 Credits of income tax paid in foreign countries can be used for reducing the tax burden in India under the DTAA (Double Taxation Avoidance Agreement) between India and other countries. Moreover, this tax credit is also available if India does not have a DTAA with the foreign country in which the buyer is investing in property. However, this is subject to some conditions.

TAX IMPLICATIONS FOR INDIANS WHILE SELLING PROPERTY ABROAD

When the property in a foreign country is sold by its Indian buyer, the gains from the transaction are subject to capital gains taxes. Long term capital gains tax is imposed at 20% after the application of indexation benefit which will be applied if the buyer held the property for more than three years. However, tax exemption can be availed on long term capital gains tax by investing the gains in other residential property in India (Section 54 of the IT Act) or by investing in NHAI/REC bonds (Section 54EC of the IT Act).

Short term capital gains tax will be applicable if the owner held the property for less than three years. This tax will be calculated on the basis of the Income Tax slab rates as ascertained to the owner. Moreover, if the capital gains are also taxed in the foreign country, DTAA can then be examined to avoid double taxation.

CHAPTER 4

IT'S TIME FOR ACTION!

With this fair and comprehensive knowledge on real estate investment, it is now time to spring into action and start searching for a real estate property. But this certainly does not mean that your first move would be to pick up the phone and start dialling every local real estate agent. Since now you do have a substantial amount of information that you might need to make the biggest investment of your lifetime, it is important to take your time and clearly understand all the knowledge provided in this book so far.

The research that you do yourself is most crucial and thus, it is highly recommended that you do adequate research before taking any decision. If you are unsure about any important aspect, rather than coming up with your own conclusions, it is better to go for professional help.

To make things easier, we will once quickly go through all the important sections of this book and then provide you with some handy tips to help you get started and keep the risks at minimum throughout the process.

WHAT HAVE YOU LEARNED SO FAR?

With all the major aspects of real estate market in India already discussed in the previous pages, let us now have a quick look at some of the most important ones.

REAL ESTATE SECTOR IN INDIA

By the year 2020, the real estate market in India will touch $180 billion as per a report from Indian Brand Equity Foundation. Government's focus on affordable housing, changes to a number of key real estate policies, FDI, and rapid development of Tier II and Tier II cities are some of the reasons that will contribute to the growth of real estate sector.

INVESTING IN REAL ESTATE

When it comes to investment in residential or commercial property, numerous crucial factors need to be considered. Understanding his/her requirement, selecting between residential and commercial properties, managing the finances, types of loans available to buy real estate property, policies and laws regarding real estate are some of the most significant factors among others.

While not every investor takes care of all of the above-mentioned factors, the whole process of investing in real estate is much simpler if you could gain the required knowledge. Moreover, modern real estate developers also offer a variety of payment plans, offers and schemes to lure investors. However, make sure that you clearly understand the deal before finalizing anything. Getting online and learning about the real estate sector before actually investing can be a much safer option than other.

MAKING MONEY WITH REAL ESTATE INVESTMENT

While the cost of property appreciates over time, a large number of investors give their property on rent to earn additional income. So, when an investor is already aware that they will be putting their property on rent, it is important to invest in properties that yield higher rent. Moreover, there are many ways that can allow you to make the property more valuable and maximize your rental income.

Apart from buying real estate property, a lot of investors consider investing in land, REIT, and by flipping multiple properties. However, these investment options require detailed information about the procedure and a bit of experience always works as an added advantage. So, before investing in these options, make sure that you have adequate knowledge about them. Rather than taking decisions on your own, professional help would make things easier and will protect you from making a wrong investment.

TAX AND REAL ESTATE INVESTMENT

Indian residents as well as NRIs are required to pay taxes on their real estate investments. There are taxes on rental income and also when you buy or sell a property in India. The Income Tax laws in respect to NRIs buying or selling a property in India are slightly different from the laws for Indian residents. Moreover, a lot of Indians too, invest in real estate properties in foreign countries. Just like Indian properties, an Indian investor is required to pay taxes on foreign properties as well. However, there are several ways in which the tax burden can be significantly reduced.

So, now that we have covered all the important aspects of investing in real estate in India, it is time to get started.

TIPS TO GET STARTED

Now that it is finally time to get things started, let us have a look at some tips that are indeed helpful.

1. AVOID GOING FOR A FIXER-UPPER

While a property that you can buy at a rate that is much lower than that of the current market rates might look very tempting, it is not really a very good idea, especially if you want to let it out for rent. To make this workable, you will need a contractor that can do high-quality work at bargain rates. Otherwise, you will end up paying a significant amount of money on renovation.

Moreover, if the quality of work is not good, the property might require repair works on a regular basis. Over time, the repair costs can accumulate to a substantial amount. If you are looking for resale flats, the right decision would be to choose one that is reasonably priced as per the market rates and needs minimum repairs.

2. CAREFULLY CHOOSE THE LOCATION

A number of smaller cities and districts are advancing at an impressive rate in India. To get best returns on your investment, try to invest in these areas. A district having a good school around, an area where the job market is flourishing, a locality with amenities like restaurants, malls, parks within close range, are some of the major criteria to make a good choice of property.

Also, make sure that you check the future plans of the local governing bodies. For instance, if they are planning to build a highway, railway station, mall, etc. in a particular area in future, real estate properties in these areas will then carry an excellent appreciation potential.

3. INVEST IN UNDER-CONSTRUCTION PROPERTY WITH CAUTION

If you are looking to invest in an under-construction property, make sure that you thoroughly check the track record of the developer along with the quality of their work. Rather than investing in a property that is being developed by a new developer, it is better to invest in properties being developed by popular builders. While you might be required to pay a slightly higher price, the investment is completely justified, as it will provide you with peace of mind about timely completion of the project.

4. SIZE OF THE FLAT

If the average cost of a 2BHK flat or apartment in a particular area is Rs. 50 lakhs and a new developer is selling a 2BHK flat at Rs. 40 lakhs, then the latter sounds as a great deal. Do not just go by the price but also check the entire details as well. Majority of the real estate advertisements do not mention the size of the flat. A 2BHK flat can be made in 2,000 sq.ft and in 800 sq.ft as well.

Jones Lang La-Salle, a popular property consultant in India, suggests in a recent report that the average size of apartments in metro cities has come down substantially in the last few years. For instance, in Mumbai alone, the average size of apartments has reduced by 31% in the last five years. Thus, make sure that you do not compare the overall costs of apartments and start looking for the price per square foot to determine whether a project is actually profitable for you or not.

The above-mentioned tips are important for every property buyer, no matter if they are buying property for the first time or are investing in one to gain returns over time.

WHEN IT'S TIME TO GET OUT, GET OUT!

Once an investor invests in a real estate property, the next step is to wait for the right time to sell it. However, there are a number of scenarios which the investor should consider before selling the property. Some of these scenarios are discussed below -

UNDERPERFORMING PROPERTY

While investors try their very best to search for properties in areas that carry good potential to appreciate in future, things do not always work as per natural order. Real estate investment requires substantial investment. Apart from the cost of the property itself, an investor is required to pay other upfront fees, like stamp duty, registration, besides regular maintenance cost of the property.

Thus, it is very important for the property to provide returns that are at par with the investment. So, how to know if a property is underperforming?

There are two important factors that can help an investor assess the performance of a property - Yield and Capital Growth.

Yield can be defined as the cash that the investor is getting from the property, that is, the income generated from rent. Capital growth is the increasing value of the investment. After calculating both, the investor can compare it with the amount invested in the property till date to know whether or not the property is actually providing the desired returns. If not, it is better to sell it and look for better options.

BETTER OPTION

Another scenario in which selling the current property can be a good decision is when an investor has a better option. If the investor has information about a property that can provide better rent or a property that has a high capital growth potential, selling the current property can be considered as a good decision. But before taking this move, the positive potentials in the other property need to be completely guaranteed.

LOSING SLEEP OVER IT

If the property on which the investor has put his money makes him panic about the profit aspects of the property, then it is better to sell it and look for better options. For instance, if an investor is struggling to find good tenants at reasonable rates, worried about whether or not the property will actually provide the desired returns, or troubled with the thought of forthcoming bathroom repair as a leakage was found on the outer wall during a recent inspection, then such properties should be got ridden off faster. Losing sleep and deteriorating life over the investment is definitely not a great option. Rather, a better alternative is to sell it and invest the money in something that does not result in any kind of distress.

Selling an investment property in the above-mentioned scenarios can be considered as a good move. While the investor might not be able to get the returns that they had expected, rather than waiting for things to change, they would be able to look for other better opportunities.

It is also very important to keep the risks at minimum while buying a property, holding it for a considerable time and then selling it. Real estate investments require huge monetary involvement and hence, it is very important to remain cautious at every step.

MINIMIZING THE RISKS

Good return is always a defining factor of real estate investment. Similar to all investments, real estate also comes with its own variety of risks. Thus, it is very important to take steps to keep risks at minimum throughout the process. Here is a list of some important tips to minimize risks while investing in real estate in India.

FOCUS ON YOUR HOMEWORK

Needless to say, investing in a real estate property is a pretty expensive affair. So, it is very important to do adequate research before taking any big step. Look for the capital growth trends, vacancy rates, and rental yields of areas where you are looking to buy a property. This will allow you to invest in areas that carry minimum risks.

CHOOSE LOAN CAREFULLY

If an investor is looking to take a home loan to buy a property, it is very important to compare the interest rates offered by different banks and other financial institutions to get the best possible rates. While there is minor difference in interest rates at which the different banks and other financial companies offer home loans, it is important to remember that the smallest of difference can have a significant impact on the total amount you repay. Lenders are eagerly looking for borrowers and there is a great negotiating opportunity to get the loan at best rates.

THINK ABOUT LONG-TERM INVESTMENT

In order for a real estate property to offer substantial returns, an investor is generally recommended to hold on to the property for at least five to eight years. While the property rates in India may seem to have risen considerably in the current times, this higher rate did not happen overnight. If you intent to sell the property too soon after buying, you would be ignoring the costs in legal fees and taxes which may actually make the entire deal non-profitable for you. Thus, if you cannot hold a property for a long time, it is better to look for other investment options.

BE SMART AFTER YOU BUY THE PROPERTY

Investors who want to rent out the property for additional rental income are often concerned about whether or not their property would find any tenant. There are actually two reasons due to which a property generally remains vacant. The property being heavily damaged or the rent being too high are usually the two reasons. Thus, it is very important to focus on proper maintenance of the property and proper research on the rental rates in the area. Make sure that you do not rely on the rental estimates provided by the seller. Rather rely on your own research.

MAINTAIN ALL THE RECORDS SYSTEMATICALLY

Create a file with all the important property documents, like the instalment receipts, copy of plan approval, commencement certificate, agreement of sale, and occupancy certificate to ensure that you have easy access to them whenever you need them.

If an investor is investing in real estate for the first time, professional help is highly recommended to avoid these risks that can prove catastrophic in future. Experienced investors too are advised to take every step cautiously as a small mistake can result in unfortunate outcomes.

REWRITING KISMET

REWRITING KISMET

BY SACHIN MITTAL

This book is not about motivation or inspiration. It's not about how to make money. It is specifically concentrated on the obstacles and impediments that crop up in any entrepreneur's passage through the tough world of business and commerce.

Among other things this book will show you how:

- God's and grandma's ideas won't make you rich any more
- In the new era the meaning of the word "commitment" has changed
- Loyalty is no longer important in the new era
- How scary it is to build something new
- Never to fear the law
- You can succeed by breaking the rules and not following common beliefs
- Your past can be your greatest strength
- Entrepreneurs should never have a back-up plan
- Your comfort zone can be the greatest enemy of your courage and confidence
- Entrepreneurs have nothing to fear but fear itself
- It's perfectly okay to be the freak, the misfit, the outcast

… and many more

HOW THE FUTURE WILL RESHAPE WORK

**ASSURED RETURNS IN
REAL ESTATE – MYTH OR REALITY**

TO BUY OR NOT TO BUY A HOME

HOW THE FUTURE WILL RESHAPE WORK

BY SACHIN MITTAL

The future of work is being enormously impacted by technological developments

as also by the growing prevalence of millennials in the workforce. It is estimated that by 2025, millennials will comprise 75% of the workforce – they will choose flexibility, freedom in their work, 100% connectivity, creativity and innovativeness over higher salaries. Work-life balance will be their mantra. They will look for and select collaborativeplatforms for working in teams, across geographical borders.

Increased mobility and globalization will change the dynamics oforganizations with employees shifting base and loyalties several times during their working life. Unlike earlier generations, the current lot of workers do not see the value in sticking to one job – rather they will take on multiple assignments and work with several employees at the same time.

Communication is on a totally new high with instant connectivity on new devices. Artificial intelligence, robotic technology and the like are transforming the face of business and work as we know it. It is time indeed for us to welcome the future of work.

This book is an account of all that ishappening and will happen in the future.

ASSURED RETURNS IN REAL ESTATE – MYTH OR REALITY

BY SACHIN MITTAL

An 'Assured Return' scheme in Real Estate is basically when a builder offers fixed monthly returns to the investor on the amount invested by him/her. A Memorandum of Understanding (MoU) is signed as a formal agreement between the builder and the investor wherein the seller promises to pay the buyer as assured sum of money each month for a specified period of time. Assured Returns on Real Estate are usually offered in either of the following three modes:

a) Assured returns till Possession
b) Assured returns till Possession + 3 years
c) Assured returns till Possession + till first lease

Such a scheme works for the builders since with excess supply in hand, their creditworthiness gets reduced in the eyes of the bank and private equity, forcing them to look towards other funding options. In case of investors, the monthly returns always work as a psychological pull.

TO BUY OR NOT TO BUY A HOME

BY SACHIN MITTAL

A home can be a place where you sleep unconscious at night, then have to leave before light, and only later will return back to the next night. So much of a person's time can be spent anywhere besides their residence. This can be one's reality. It is for so many professionals working in major cities in India, those who work in the travel industry and others who work outside the home.

A home can also be a place of work; a place where one spends most of one's time. This is especially true for the stay-at-home parent, extended family, or the professional who is permitted to work out of his or her home remotely. Many freelancers work out of the home these days, in fact.

Times are changing. People's needs are changing—particularly when it comes to how one comes to think of their home.

This book has been written for the individual seeking their own place to call home. A residence to live in that will foster future memories, assist one to have a better quality of life, and ensure one has a place to rest unconscious at night, before returning back to consciousness come the following morning.